JOURNEYS INTO BRECON'S PAST

Journeys into Brecon's Past

W. S. K. Thomas

First impression—November 1996

ISBN 1 85902 386 X

© W. S. K. Thomas

Printed by Gomer Press, Llandysul, Dyfed

I
Brian
ffrind fy mebyd

Contents

Preface

This is a book that 'just happened'. I had completed my planned trilogy on the history of Brecon, and was hoping to allow my pen, for a while at least, to remain in a condition of 'suspended animation'. Suddenly, upon seeing the countless hordes wandering, rather aimlessly, through the streets and lanes of the ancient borough, an idea impressed itself on my mind. Why not provide a greater purpose and meaning to their visit by steering them to places of considerable historic interest? In a sense, therefore, this is a guide-book, but a guide-book with a difference. I make no apology for departing from the more traditional methods of writing local history, and I can only hope that the reader will endorse my rather unconventional approach.

Writing history is a most pleasurable and fulfilling experience in itself, but it acquires an added dimension when one is brought into contact, albeit not physically, with others who have toiled in the same field. It is only then that one's indebtedness to their labours becomes fully appreciated, and it is with considerable satisfaction that I record my gratitude to these researchers. Hopefully, the fruits of my efforts will meet with their approval.

In writing this volume I contracted my usual obligation to Emeritus Professor Glanmor Williams who, recently, to the unmitigated joy and satisfaction of his numerous friends and admirers, was awarded a knighthood for his services to Welsh History, Welsh Culture and the Welsh Language. Sir Glanmor Williams, who was my teacher in my undergraduate days, and has been a guide and mentor ever since, was kind enough to read this book in typescript with his usual meticulous care, and his wisdom and scholarship enabled me to avoid many of the pitfalls strewn along the way. I acknowledge my debt to him with considerable warmth and satisfaction. Needless to say I hold myself entirely responsible for any errors of fact or interpretation that still remain.

Colleagues of mine from Brecon High School days are also deserving of my gratitude: Mr Stanley Foulkes and Mrs Eira G. Jones for their painstaking reading of the proofs, and Dr W. Ll. Williams for his reconstruction of a Celtic church and the maps on pages xviii and 84. My thanks are also owing to another companion, Mr Glanville Francis Thomas, for his constant encouragement when the spirit was flagging. I wish to acknowledge, as well, the support I received from Dr John Alban, Swansea City Archivist.

During the course of writing the book I visited many libraries and museums, especially those at Brecon, and to the staffs of these institutions I am deeply indebted. I particularly want to thank Mr David Moore of Brecknock Museum, and Mr Christopher Price of Brecon Library, for their monumental patience and undiminished enthusiasm in hunting down old prints, photographs and publications which I urgently needed. It is also a considerable pleasure to record my thanks to Dr Dyfed Elis-Gruffydd of Gomer Press for his understanding, and unfailing courtesy, when guiding the book through the various stages of publication.

Finally, my long-suffering wife and family deserve special mention. Only too recently they were required to entertain many of Brecknock's notabilities under the family roof, and no sooner had Sarah Siddons, Adelina Patti, Howell Harris and the others departed than they were invited to proceed with me on journeys of discovery into Brecon's past. However, these trials and tribulations were borne with commendable fortitude and patience, and without their encouragement and active support this volume would never have seen the light of day.

Illustrations

Maps

Introduction

Whilst my last book, *Footprints in the Sand,* dealt with personalities, the present volume, while introducing more of Brecon's notabilities to the reader, is basically about places. When the casual visitor looks around Brecon and her environs, he cannot but be made aware of, and be impressed by, the wealth of historical remains and monuments which everywhere abound. Prehistoric hill-forts, Roman camps, Norman castles, manor houses, churches, together with a monastery here and a friary there, dot the landscape; manifestations in stone of man's resourcefulness and ingenuity, and his yearning for self-preservation and spiritual comfort.

In the caves at Dan-yr-ogof near Craig-y-nos, Stone Age man found a fairly secure refuge for himself and his family, and nearby, archaeologists have recently uncovered evidence of Bronze Age settlements. The Celts, with their Iron Age culture, left permanent and very visible imprints on the landscape in their hill-fort camps like the one at Pen-y-crug overlooking the town of Brecon, and in the crannog at Llangorse there is evidence of Celtic lake-dwellers. The Roman invader, apart from building a countrywide grid of excellent roads, constructed forts and towns. At the Gaer, a few miles to the north-west of Brecon, there is located a substantial auxiliary fort, outside which a civic settlement grew, and Roman soldiers stationed there married local girls.

The Roman legions left these shores in 410 A.D. because the barbarian hordes were hammering at the very gates of the eternal city, Rome. Their departure was followed by other waves of invaders as the Angles, Saxons, and Jutes poured across the English Channel from the Continent. Following the remorseless drive of these Anglo-Saxons westwards, the Celts in Strathclyde in the north, and those in Devon and Cornwall in the south, became separated from their fellow Celts in Wales, though from the fifth to the eighth centuries the Christians amongst the Celts maintained contact with one another, and founded semi-monastic *clas* churches like the one at Llanddew near Brecon.

However, the Saxons never succeeded in pushing their conquests to the Irish Sea, and the independence of the Celts in Wales was not to be seriously threatened until the Norman Conquest of 1066. The situation now changed, and from about 1070 onwards, the Norman knights, operating from border strongholds such as Gloucester, Hereford, Shrewsbury and Chester, gradually pushed into Wales via the river valleys, and they carved out virtually autonomous kingdoms for themselves by defeating the local Welsh princes and chieftains and usurping their territories and sovereign rights. Brecknock was to witness the unwelcomed arrival of Bernard de Newmarch and his followers from Hereford, and as these Norman *conquistadores* moved ever further westwards into the kingdom, they riveted their control over the conquered lands by building castles of the motte and bailey type at various strategic points. At Bronllys, a fortification was built on a rock outcrop overlooking the confluence of the Dulais and Llynfi rivers, while at Brecon, after his resounding victory over the local Welsh, presumably at Battle, Bernard finished the construction of his *caput*, or head, castle on a spur of land above the rivers Usk and Honddu. Within bowshot of his castle, Bernard endowed a Benedictine Priory, and the ranks of the regular clergy were further augmented in the thirteenth century by the building of the Dominican friary of St. Nicholas in the suburb of Llanfaes. To the south-east of Brecon, at Tretower, another of Bernard's followers, Picard, about 1100, built a castle on a site which enabled him to control movement up the Rhiangoll and Usk valleys. This fortification was to be occupied by the family for upwards of two hundred years. The castle was abandoned as a residence in the early fourteenth century, and with considerations of greater domestic comfort in mind, in a politically more stable society, a fortified manor house was built nearby. In the fifteenth century the house was acquired through gift by the Vaughan family, the most notable member of which was Henry Vaughan, the Silurist, who was inspired by the deep solitude and ethereal beauty of the locality, and his passionate love of the river Usk, to pen magical lines of verse.

But the Welsh did not relinquish their independence lightly. They fought as well as they could against a better-armed, mounted foe, and in the thirteenth century, two of the princes of Gwynedd attempted to unify Wales and create a feudal state along similar lines to those that existed in contemporary England and France. Llywelyn ap Iorwerth and his grandson, Llywelyn ap Gruffydd, both failed in their aspirations, and at Cilmery, near Builth, as a permanent memorial, there stands a massive granite monolith near the spot where the last prince of Wales, *Llywelyn ein Llyw Olaf*, was slain in 1282, striving valiantly to turn the tide of Anglo-Norman conquest and domination.

Considerable attention in this narrative is also devoted to the substantial houses of the gentry. An impressive dwelling still in Glamorgan Street is Buckingham Place, a late sixteenth- and early seventeenth-century house, probably built by Dr Awbrey of Abercynrig. Through the centuries eminent people have resided there, and in their ranks have been bishops such as Dr William Lucy of St David's, members of Parliament like Howel Gwyn and Cyril Flower, and a formidable champion of women's rights, Gwenllian Morgan. In the realm of local government Miss Morgan has to be credited with two major triumphs: she was the first woman in Brecon and Wales to become an elected councillor, and the first to be elevated to the office of mayor. Indeed, Gwenllian Morgan helped to blaze a trail which led eventually to the complete emancipation of women. Priory House, adjoining the Cathedral, is another edifice most worthy of attention as its occupants and guests have included worthies like Sir John Price, the author of the first book to be printed and published in Welsh, *Yny Lhyvyr Hwnn*, in 1546, Charles I in 1645 following his disastrous defeat at Naseby by Oliver Cromwell, and George IV in 1821 when his dinner was prepared by a Mrs Edwards, the wife of Jonathan Edwards, the manager of the Castle of Brecon Hotel. Other substantial houses visited are Newton, the ancestral home in Llanfaes of the Games family, and Penoyre, the residence of Colonel J. Lloyd Vaughan Watkins, the liberal member of Parliament for Brecon, and an active proponent of parliamentary reform.

Following the dissolution of the friary in 1538, an endowed grammar school known as the College of Christ, or Christ College, was established on the site by Bishop William Barlow in 1541. Between 1541 and 1853 the school had a rather chequered history, as there were quite violent fluctuations in its fortunes. A great turning-point was the enactment in 1853 of the Christ College Act of Parliament. Consequent upon the passing of this legislation a modern public school, with its own board of governors, came into existence in 1855. Far reaching changes rapidly followed, including a substantial building programme which made possible the admission of more pupils, and the character of the curriculum was considerably altered. However, in the late nineteenth century, following the passing of the Welsh Intermediate Act 1889, a state system of secondary schools was placed in position, and at Brecon a purpose-built grammar school for boys, on which some attention will be focused, was opened in Cradoc Road in 1901, and another for the girls on Cerrig Cochion Hill at the same time.

The arteries of trade and commerce are given due prominence, and the Turnpike road leading through the Watton, and the drovers' road over the Epynt, kindle the imagination. And in the Watton, running parallel with the road for a short distance, is to be found the Brecon to Abergavenny canal, along which coal, lime, and agricultural products were conveyed by barge. In Breconshire, with its numerous rivers and streams, and heavy rainfall, bridges were of cardinal importance, and some of these bridges were very substantial structures and quite picturesque. Such is the bridge which links the town with its suburb of Llanfaes, over which both English and Welsh poets have enthused.

Along these turnpike roads English theatre companies from the border counties would arrive at Brecon for a season. One such company was established by John Ward, and in May and June 1755, it played for the entire eight weeks. It was during this protracted stay that Sarah Siddons, who was to become the greatest tragédienne ever to have graced the boards in this country, was born in a local inn. These strolling players used inns, or theatres attached to them, for the presentation of their art, and one such theatre was the 'Theatre Royal' in the Watton. At these playhouses the urban gentry were entertained, and without this 'genteel' patronage the provincial theatre would not have been able to exist at all.

Other objects of attention include the new Shire Hall built in the Doric style of architecture, and completed in 1842. It was here, until 1971, that the Assizes were held, when felons were either committed to the county gaol situated in the western extremity of Llanfaes, or ordered to be publicly hanged before its walls. Since Brecon, from Roman days, has had close associations with the military, it is obviously appropriate to devote attention to the barracks from where dragoons were dispatched in the 1830s, a decade of intense social and political unrest in Wales, to quell riots at Merthyr, Llanidloes, Newport and Carmarthen.

Though Brecon is an ancient market town it has, periodically, flirted with industrialisation. In 1720, on the banks of the Honddu, a furnace and forge were established, and since there were no iron deposits in Brecon, the iron ore had to be transported there on the backs of horses from Hirwaun, some eighteen miles away. The works were not of long duration, and by 1800 silence had once again descended on the banks of the river. But this suburb of Brecon was not finished with industrialism yet, because in 1920, Harold Elston, by harnessing the Honddu torrent, was able to establish a hydro-electric plant in his garage in the Struet, and cables were laid to enable him to light adjacent premises. Furthermore, adjoining his garage, was a brewery where a fine ale was produced, and at Priory Hill, only a short distance away, a woollen mill was situated. Today, since electrical power to drive machinery is so readily available, the industrial face of Brecon has been transformed. It was not on the banks of the Honddu that a modern industrial estate was located, but rather at Ffrwdgrech to the west of the town.

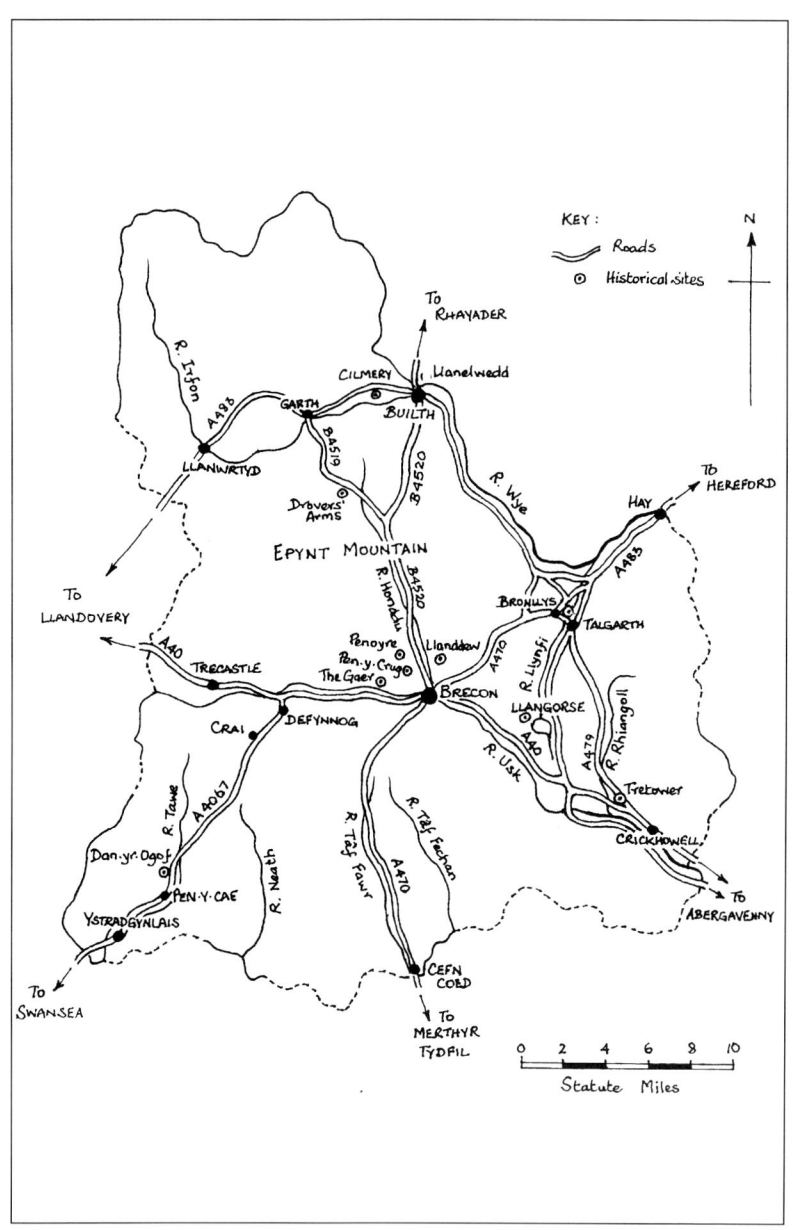

Location of places of historical interest visited outside Brecon.

Day 1: Pen-y-Crug, the Gaer and Llanddew; Giraldus Cambrensis

On a hill overlooking the town of Brecon, at a thousand feet above sea-level, stands the Celtic hill-fort of Pen-y-Crug. Fort is really a misnomer because Pen-y-Crug, like many other Celtic hill-forts in Wales, was in fact a defended settlement. Within it people lived and worked, gave birth and died, and death could be swift and violent.

Some time during the fourth century B.C., as part of a great folk movement, the Celts, a warlike, iron-using people, had invaded the British isles from the Continent, and they had pushed inland via the river valleys. Wales received some of these newcomers, traders and settlers alike, from south-west England. The Celts came in three successive waves, and a substantial number of the hill-forts of Wales belong to the second phase of penetration, about the second century B.C. The tribesmen who built the hill-forts at Brecon, Y Fenni, Slwch, and elsewhere in Brecknock, had entered the county via the Usk, Llynfi and Rhiangoll basins; and this pattern of settlement is demonstrated quite clearly by the geographical disposition of the forts since they are located in or immediately around the rich agricultural land associated with these regions.

The fort at Brecon is to be found one and a quarter miles to the north-west of the town on a moorland hilltop. To reach it we follow the B4520 road north of the borough for a mile before treading a path on the west side of the road to the Crug. The fort, oval in shape, is about 600 feet in length and about 430 feet in width, and is provided with three sloping inner ramparts and two weaker outward ramparts tiered around the top of the hill. These ramparts, consisting of earth and rubble thrown out when the ditches were dug, and probably faced internally and externally with rough coursed masonry, are massive. Even now, in their collapsed state, the tops of the main ramparts are, in places, nearly twenty feet above the base of their ditches. This arrangement ideally suited the needs of the slingers standing on the parapet of the innermost rampart. The passageway leading up to the entrance, which is situated to the south-east, is long and narrow, making an assault by

1

An aerial view of Pen-y-Crug hill-fort.

large numbers on the gateway extremely difficult and hazardous. The entrance is further strengthened by the fact that it is flanked by successive inturns of the ramparts. An annexe outside the entrance is, quite possibly, the remains of an earlier fort.

The existence of such a formidable camp at Pen-y-Crug is doubtless indicative that the tribesmen had become agriculturists, since in the agricultural stage life tended to become more stabilised, and the old nomadic habits either fell into disuse, or were carried on only by a section of the tribe. The adoption of agriculture led to the families forming some permanent settlement near the arable lands whilst the herds would be left in the care of children. These herders would have continued to accompany the animals in their seasonal migrations from winter pastures on lower plateaux to summer pastures on the higher ones, from *hendre* to *hafod,* but the remainder of the community would have remained at the permanent home, the *hendre.* The tribe could now accumulate wealth in bulk and, as a consequence, would need some safe retreat especially in times of trouble. Such a haven could be provided by a defensive enclosure like a hill-fort. Significantly, excavations at other hill-fort sites have revealed the presence of corn, iron sickles, stone querns

2

for grinding, and ploughshares. However, despite these interesting finds, very little is known about Iron Age culture in Wales, for very few of these hill-forts have been excavated. The archaeologist is further considerably handicapped by the fact that the wet climate of Wales has proved most unhelpful, as corrosion has either destroyed or hopelessly disfigured the iron tools and weapons lying in the soil. The student of these settlements has to work from crumbs of evidence.

The greater stability, together with the manpower required to build these mammoth earthworks—and their construction would have been accompanied by a substantial clearance of woodland— are forceful arguments in favour of regarding these camps as permanent residences. The primary purpose, after all, was defensive; and a chieftain, with a small band of warriors or retainers, would undoubtedly have resided there together with a substantial number of tribesmen. But the camps also served as places of refuge for those free tribesmen who lived outside on the fringes of the forest. The chieftain would have been central to the whole community since such an authoritarian figure was necessary to control arrangements within the camp and to organise the defences in times of danger. However, there were camps in Brecknockshire which were never intended as centres of permanent human habitation. These were built on the slopes of hills, their defences were weak—the common arrangement was two banks and a ditch—and they were dominated by the higher ground behind. The purpose of these hill-slope camps could not possibly have been military, and it has been suggested[1] that they were used as kraals by the tribesmen to protect their animals such as oxen, sheep, goats, and pigs at night from cattle raiders and from ravaging foxes, bears, and wolves.

From excavations at other sites it can be assumed that within the defensive ramparts and ditches, the tribesmen at Pen-y-Crug lived in huts which were predominantly circular in shape, though some could have been rectangular. These early builders used whatever materials were available locally and, at Brecon, timber and stone would have been found in abundance. The beehive huts could have been built entirely of mud and wattle, or they could have consisted of a stone wall built to a height of three or four feet on which were placed posts, encompassing a central pole, supporting a conical roof. The roof would have been formed of rushes, turves, heather, or even stone. The dwellings were provided with hearths, located in the centre—the central pole being shielded from the fire by a stone slab—or against a wall, though there is some evidence that some of the cooking, presumably of the larger animals, was done outside. Some of the hearths were built up, whilst others consisted of oval hollows in the floor. Whatever the plan adopted, these habitations would have had very smoky interiors, and they would have been cold, draughty, and wet. As a consequence the tribesmen, during part of the year at least, would have suffered from some ailment or other. Further, as there was only the one room, it would have had to function as living room, larder, kitchen, bedroom, and workshop.

A hill-fort. (courtesy of National Museum of Wales)

The tribesmen who built the hill-fort at Pen-y-Crug were Brythons, a small dark people who spoke a language called British. These Britons or Celts were the direct ancestors of the modern Welsh people, and their language the precursor of Welsh. Very little is known about the ancient British tongue, as there are no written texts extant in the language. All one can say is that the language was probably in a state of evolution, and in the period of social upheaval following the departure of the Roman legions in 410 A.D., the process of change would have been accelerated. By the second half of the sixth century a new language had been born, and that language was unmistakably Welsh.

The Gaer

We now retrace our footsteps to the B4520 and pursue the road north for about a mile before turning left for Cradoc. From Cradoc we proceed to Aberyscir and the Roman camp located nearby.

The Romans first landed on the shores of Britain in 55 B.C., though this expedition, led by Julius Caesar, was in the nature of a military reconnaissance. The following year, 54 B.C., he came again, but on this occasion he was much better prepared. He defeated the Belgae, pursued them across the river Thames, and captured their stronghold at *Verulam* (St Albans). Following this success, he withdrew to Gaul.

Almost a century was to elapse before the Romans reappeared in 43 A.D. Conquest was rapid, and by 49 A.D. the Second Legion was stationed at Gloucester (*Glevum*). The Roman thrust south and west was now blunted by the stern opposition offered by the Silures, with whom Caratacus (Caradog), the son of Cunobelinus, had taken shelter after the capture of Colchester. It was not until *c.* 75 A.D. that the Silures were overcome by Julius Frontinus, the governor of Britain (74-78 A.D.), and the Second Legion advanced to a new fortress at Caerleon (*Isca*). The conquest of north Wales was completed three years later by Julius Agricola, the succeeding governor, and he had operated from a new legionary base at Chester (*Deva*).

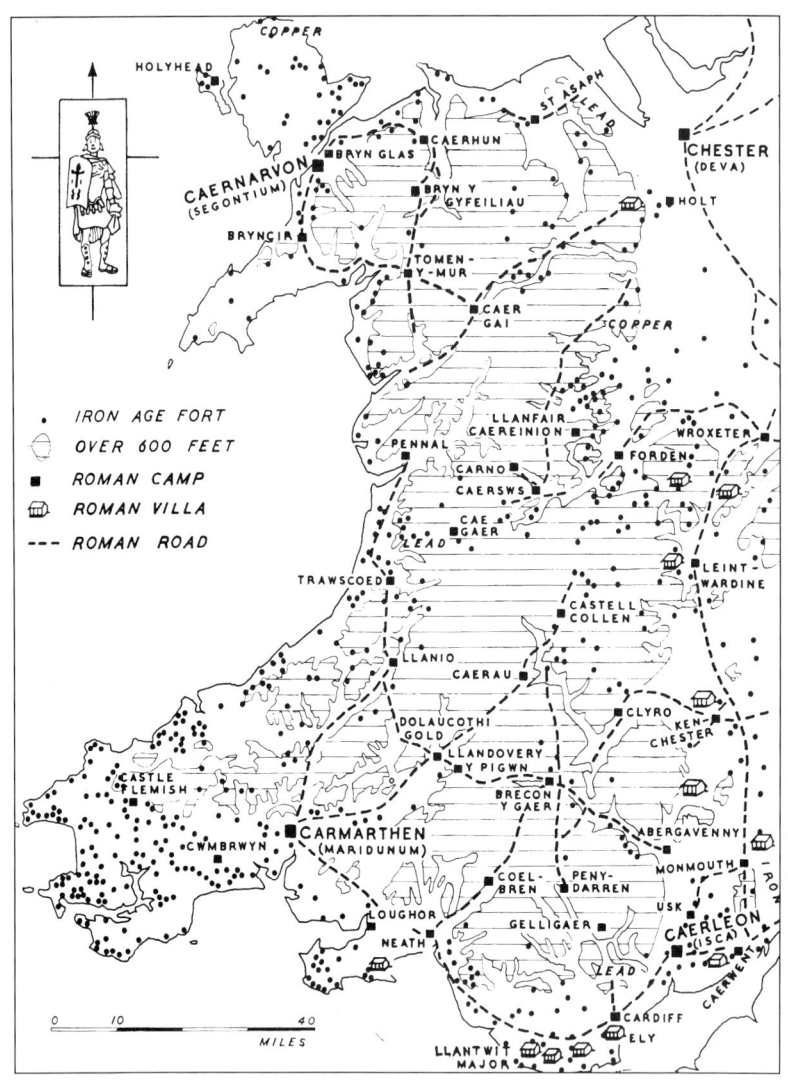

Roman Wales.

The Roman strategy for the subjugation of Wales was to establish forts at strategic points, all connected by a network of roads slung between Chester and Caerleon on the east and Caernarvon and Carmarthen in the west. None of the forts was more than a day's march from another so that assistance was readily available when trouble brewed. The legionary fortresses at Chester and Caerleon, which housed the Twentieth and Second Legions respectively, were huge, since they each embraced an area of some fifty acres. Within their massive ramparts 6,000 highly trained men, all Roman citizens, were quartered. The forts, on the other hand, were normally of between three to six acres, and occupied by auxiliary troops. These could consist of an *ala* of cavalry or a cohort of infantry some of whom could well have been mounted, with a nominal strength of 1,000 or five hundred men recruited from the provinces of the Roman empire.

The Gaer (*Cicutium*) was one of those forts manned by auxiliaries, and the largest of its kind in Wales. It was probably established *c*. 75 A.D., and was strategically positioned where the east-west road from Abergavenny to Llandovery crossed the north-south road between Castell Collen, near Llandrindod Wells, and Neath. Another road branched south to Gelligaer, six miles north of Caerphilly. From part of a tombstone found near Battle, about a mile to the north of the Gaer, it has been possible to establish that about 100 A.D., the fort was garrisoned by an *ala* of Vettonian Spanish cavalry. The inscription, restorations being given in italics, reads as follows: 'Dis. M*anibus* Cand*id*i . . . Ni. Fili *eq alae* Hisp. Vett *c. r.* Clem. Dom*itius* . . . *her.* An. xx. Stip. III. H. *s.e*'.[2]

The camp at Aberyscir embraced an area of eight acres and, in common with other Roman camps in Wales, was rectangular in plan, though with rounded corners like playing cards. Originally, the defences were of earth and timber and comprised a bank and two ditches, whilst the gateways and interior buildings were constructed of wood. During the first decade of the second century, when the Romans overhauled their Welsh frontier defences, the Gaer was reconstructed. The bank was faced with stone and heightened, and the gates and principal buildings were rebuilt in masonry. The excellence of the work and the design of the

Tombstone found near Battle.

Aerial view of the Gaer.

gateways, together with the fact that tiles have been found on the site bearing the stamp of the Second Legion, would seem to suggest that both men and material from Caerleon were used in the work of restructuring. However, the work was never completed, and the barrack-blocks were never rebuilt in stone.

The camp at Brecon was very short-lived; it had an active life of only some sixty years. After *c*. 140 A.D. there is no evidence to suggest other than that it was possibly occupied by an official caretaker, who could have been an old soldier living on a pension, though doubtless the fort was visited occasionally by a patrol from Caerleon. The explanation is to be found in the need for its garrison to fight in the north of England, where it undoubtedly assisted in the construction of two walls to keep out the warring Picts who were conducting destructive forays from Scotland: one was Hadrian's Wall running from the Tyne to the Solway, while the other was the Antonine Wall. It is hardly surprising, therefore, to discover the Vettonian cavalry at Bowes in the North Riding of Yorkshire and at Binchester in County Durham. The new bath-house, built inside the fort, and replacing a larger original one outside, was undoubtedly intended to cater for the needs of a skeleton garrison.

The Gaer was provided with four gateways facing north, south, east and west. The west gate, built on entirely more monumental lines, was undoubtedly the principal entrance. It consisted of a double carriageway flanked by two guardrooms or towers, which projected for nearly half their width beyond the line of the fort wall. The designs of the other gates were roughly similar, though the guardrooms were built on the line of the fort wall.

Apart from the new baths, the buildings were constructed on the east side of the street running from north to south. Immediately adjoining this street were the granary, the headquarters building (*Principia*), and the commandant's house (*Praetorium*). The granary was heavily buttressed to sustain the weight of stores within. The headquarters building, north of which was a well, consisted of halls ranged around the sides of a courtyard. A series of rooms opened off the near hall, the central one housing the regimental treasure and shrine. Before this building was a large fore-hall or enclosure, 147 feet long and 40 feet wide, which may possibly have been used

9

as a riding school. To the south of the headquarters building was the commandant's house, which comprised four ranges of rooms grouped again around a courtyard, with an annexe, possibly a kitchen, added on the west side.

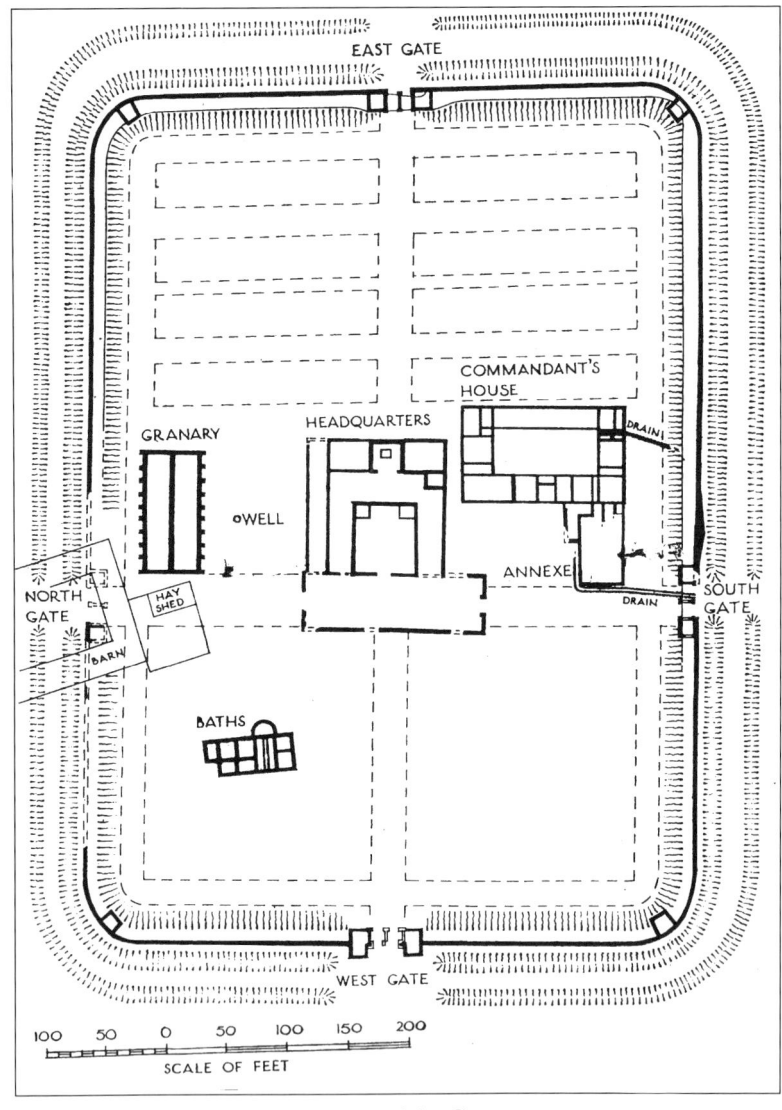

Site plan of the Gaer..

10

The eastern half of the fort was filled with barrack-blocks built of timber. There would appear to have been eight in all, each about 180 feet in length and 30 feet in breadth, and ranged in pairs facing inwards on the side streets. Normally, each barrack-block accommodated an infantry unit of eighty men or two cavalry troops, each of thirty men. The presence of eight rather than six blocks is indicative of their having been designed to house cavalry rather than infantry. Though from the size of the fort it could have been expected to hold 1,000 men, the Vettonian Spanish cavalry, which was based there, had a paper strength of 500 men.

The bath-building, which occupied the north-west corner of the fort, was stone built and supplied with the usual hot and cold rooms, together with an apsidal cold plunge. The furnace room was located at the north end, and heating was provided through a system known as the hypocaust, or under-floor heating. Bath-buildings like these, which were not part of the original design, were sometimes known as 'officers' baths' to distinguish them from the 'soldiers' baths' outside the fort. At the Gaer this explanation does not fit the case, and it is more than likely that these baths, which were intruded later (*c.* 120 A.D.), were built when the original bath-building outside the fort was abandoned because it was too large for the needs of a greatly reduced garrison.

Protection for these buildings was provided in the first instance by an earth bank five feet high and eighteen feet wide, outside which were two ditches each about six feet deep and fifteen feet wide. This bank was later raised and faced with a stone wall. The wall was three and a half feet wide, and consisted of rubble and squared sandstone blocks. It now stands to a maximum height of eleven feet. At each of the rounded corners of the fort small rectangular internal turrets were added to strengthen the defences.

During the period of intense occupation of the fort, a village of quite considerable size had grown up outside the northern defences. On both sides of the road leading from the north gate, for a distance of about three hundred yards, there were timber hutments with clay floors. However, amongst them, were at least three buildings of stone—a small shop or workshop, a building which may have been the principal bath-house, and a large residence or hostel, which could well have been occupied by the commandant's family, or used as a rest-house for official travellers. These civil settlements were inhabited by the families of the garrison—some of the soliders, at least, would have married local girls—by retired veterans, and by native tradesmen. Clearly, the existence of this settlement outside the parameters of the fort implies a pacified district. The Silures were no longer a foe to be feared, and a permanent garrison at Aberyscir could be expected to live in tolerable safety and reasonable comfort.

Following the departure of the Roman legions from Britain in 410 A.D. to defend Rome from barbarian onslaughts from the north, and long after the fort had fallen into ruins, the rampart on the north, east, and south was heightened with earth and rubble, and the east and south gates were blocked. This work could have been undertaken just prior to the Norman conquest of Brycheiniog, and the Gaer, *Caerbannau,* might well have been the fortress and residence of Bleddyn ap Maenarch, the local chieftain. In 1093 Bleddyn, together with his overlord and brother-in-law, Rhys ap Tewdwr, the King of Deheubarth, was killed by the Normans at Battle.

Llanddew—Church and Episcopal Palace

Having sensed in the imagination, if only for a comparatively short period, what life must have been like at the Gaer in Roman times—the hustle, bustle and frenetic activity associated with an important garrison fort so dramatically different from the peaceful tranquillity and serenity which characterise the area today—we now retrace our footsteps to the B4520. We follow the road back towards Brecon for a short distance before turning left on to a narrow lane which takes us to the small village of Llanddew. Here, awaiting us, are two objects of considerable historical interest, one in a fine state of preservation, but the other roofless and a sorry ruin where nature has been left very largely to reclaim her own. The former is the ancient parish church of St David, whilst the other is the episcopal palace, in the Middle Ages an impressive castellated mansion belonging to the bishops of the see.

Llanddew Church.

There has been considerable speculation concerning the orthography and meaning of 'Llanddew'. It has been suggested, and amongst the proponents of this theory is Giraldus Cambrensis himself, that the correct form of the word is 'Llan-Duw' (The Church of the Holy Trinity), but there are powerful objections to this interpretation from those who maintain that the correct form of the word is 'Llanddewi' (The Church of David). Ignoring the niceties of the argument, however, what is certain is that the church can claim to be one of the oldest in the county of Brecknock and, furthermore, it was the parish church of Gerald, who was archdeacon of Brecon between 1175 and 1203.

It is possible that over the centuries at least three churches have occupied the site. The first mention of a church there relates to 500 A.D., when Eluned, the twenty-third of Brychan's progeny of twenty-four saintly daughters, found refuge there. This church was probably built of wattle and daub and, as a consequence, no traces of it now remain. Undoubtedly, the church owed its appearance to the missionary zeal of a Celtic saint. During the period of Roman

13

occupation there had been very few Christians in Wales, and what archaeological evidence does exist concerning their existence relates to south-eastern Wales. Following the withdrawal of the legions, Christianity was reintroduced into the country from Gaul by way of the western sea-routes, and the Celtic church was born. Between the fifth and the eighth centuries Christianity was spread over the whole country by peripatetic monks of this church who, judging by the evidence provided by the location of gravestones, and the situation of the churches, appear to have pursued their way inland along the old Roman roads. The saint (or monk), during his wanderings, would halt at a chosen spot where he would erect a simple cross and commence preaching to the people. If success attended his efforts, a tiny wooden church would be built, which usually bore the name of the saint who first established it. Providing that the church was well situated, a small village or hamlet would, in the course of time, spring up around it. It is more than possible that it was in this rather prosaic manner that Llanddew made its first appearance.

An artist's impression of a Celtic church.

Following the missionary phase, religious life in Wales revolved around the *clas* church. The *clas* was a community of canons living in monastic buildings at whose head was an abbot. They shared responsibility for worship and pastoral work, and the church and its revenues were also divided amongst them. Marriage was permitted, and the children of such unions could inherit their father's share in the church. The *clas* was essentially a mother church and would have a number of subsidiary chapels acknowledging its authority. Furthermore, it exercised control over established territorial limits. The church at Llanddew was such a church.

There is slight architectural evidence to suggest that another church, built of stone, and possibly pre-Norman, then occupied the site. The remains of the lintel of a substantial door (*c.* 1020) are to be found in the south porch, and a piscina (a stone basin for the washing of communion vessels) of the same period is located in the south transept. However, it can be postulated with confidence that the structure which so bravely challenges the elements today is basically Early English Gothic, probably of thirteenth-century date, though it has undergone many changes and alterations. It is cruciform in shape, has no aisles, and is richly provided with tall, slender lancet windows with wide splays inside. The church is not buttressed, but the lower portions of the walls are splayed outwards which serves the same purpose. In the south wall of the chancel there is a priest's door which is trefoiled under a pointed arch. At the beginning of the nineteenth century the church was dark and dirty, and the floor was earthen and uneven. Arising from the practice of burying the dead within its walls, there was a musty smell pervading the whole building. A short, squat tower, which originally housed four bells, though these have now been reduced to two, straddles the centre of the building. From a stone placed high on the east wall of the tower, it appears that it was rebuilt in 1629, and during this decade also considerable work was carried out on the nave. But the church, in common with other churches in the area, was to suffer greatly from neglect, and by 1875 the chancel, tower, and transepts were all sealed off, only the nave being left in use. However, in the 1880s and again in the 1890s, and arising from the regeneration of church life which occurred after

1840, restoration was undertaken to enable the building to be fully used again. It was during the course of the earlier restoration that paintings and religious texts were discovered beneath the whitewash on the chancel walls which, probably, had been first applied during the reign of the Protestant Edward VI (1547-53) to obscure the medieval frescos. On the north wall portions of the Lord's Prayer in Welsh were uncovered, and the literary evidence suggests that they were placed there shortly after the translation of the complete Bible into Welsh by bishop William Morgan in 1588.

Ruins of the Episcopal Palace at Llanddew.

Across the road from the church are located the ruins of Llanddew Palace. An episcopal manor-house had stood there in the twelfth century where Giraldus Cambrensis (Gerald the Welshman) lived when he was archdeacon of Brecon. Bishop Henry Gower of St David's (1278?-1347)[3] rebuilt this house c. 1340, and it was used as a residence by the bishops and dignitaries of the diocese when they visited the district. John Leland, when he undertook his celebrated itinerary of Henry VIII's Kingdom in the 1530s, described the palace as an 'unseemly ruin'. Following the triumph of Parliament over the King in the English Civil Wars, the palace and its manors (lands) were forcibly acquired by the victorious Puritans, and, in

1658, the Puritan authorities sold them to David Morgan of Bovingdon in Hertfordshire for the very considerable sum of £546 7*s*. 1*d*. However, following the restoration of Charles II to the English throne in 1660, the palace and lands were restored to the church. Through their stewards, the bishops had held annually at Llanddew two manorial courts: the Court Leet and the Court Baron.

From Samuel Buck's engraving of 1741 we gather that substantial portions of the palace were still standing. Edwin Poole in 1886 described the site as oblong in shape and occupying an area of one and a quarter acres. It was bounded on the north and west by walls which were in a dilapidated state, on the east by a hedge, and on the south by part of the old wall and the remains of a handsome Gothic arch. In the western wall was a fine well, arched over, and so constructed within the wall that both the inmates of the palace and the villagers outside could draw its waters. In the north considerable sections of the hall block walls were still standing. The north wall extended for forty-seven feet, and contained portions of three lancet windows. There was a lancet, also, in each of the pine ends. Today, as a result of further neglect, and the ravages of time, still less remains. The arch, well, and wall in the south and west are still visible, and three of the hall walls stand tall, in places to a height of some twenty feet. Irreparable damage was done to the site in 1869, when a vicarage was built on the spot. All traces of other habitations have long since disappeared. Undoubtedly, the building materials for the vicarage were obtained from the site itself, since there was a veritable quarry of ready-dressed stone lying around.

It was on this site that one of the most colourful and flamboyant personalities of the medieval church in Wales, Giraldus Cambrensis or Gerald the Welshman, had a home. In fact, he found living there most congenial, and he was to aver that 'in these temperate regions I have obtained a place of dignity, but no great omen of future pomp or riches; and possessing a small residence near the castle of Brycheiniog, well adapted to literary pursuits, and to the contemplation of eternity, I envy not the riches of Croesus; happy and contented with that mediocrity, which I prize far beyond all the perishable and transitory things of this world'.

Monument of Giraldus Cambrensis.

Gerald was born in Manorbier castle, Pembroke, *c.* 1146 and he described his place of birth as being 'the most delectable spot in the whole of Wales'. He was a man of mixed race, for the blood of Welsh princes and Norman lords ran in his veins, his father being William de Barri, whilst his mother was Angharad, who was descended from the line of Rhys ap Tewdwr, the King of Deheubarth.

Even as a young boy Gerald had aspired to Holy Orders, and his ambitions in that direction were fostered by his uncle David Fitzgerald, the bishop of St David's. To prepare him for his chosen career he received the best education that could be provided at that time. He was sent, initially, to the great abbey of St Peter in Gloucester where his tutor was the renowned Hamo. This was to prepare him for entry into Paris university, the greatest centre of learning in Europe. On completion of his seven-year course at the university in 1174, he returned to Wales, and through the influence which his uncle, David, was able to exercise, he accumulated livings. However, he first became acquainted with Brecknock when he received a commission from Richard, the archbishop of

Canterbury, to enforce the payment of tithes on wool and cheese within the diocese. Whilst at Brecon he discovered that Jordan, the elderly archdeacon, was publicly keeping a concubine contrary to canon law. Despite being ordered by Gerald to set the woman aside, Jordan obstinately refused, and for this act of defiance he was removed from his benefice and Gerald installed in his place. Gerald was later to acknowledge that the manner in which he had obtained his office was not altogether to his credit.

It was in his capacity as archdeacon, and self-appointed champion of the bishopric of St David's, that he successfully thwarted the attempt by Adam, bishop of St Asaph, to assert his right over the church of Kerry in Montgomeryshire. The confrontation took place in the churchyard. Following a heated argument there between Gerald and the bishop over their respective claims to the church, the bishop had finally alighted from his horse and, having donned his vestments, proceeded solemnly to excommunicate Gerald. The archdeacon, not to be outdone, then excommunicated the bishop and, as confirmation of the act, he ordered the church bells to be rung three times. At this, much discomfited, the bishop remounted his horse and, together with his retinue, withdrew. As they departed they were pursued by a vast crowd who pelted them with clods of earth and stones.

Gerald had two great goals in life: one was to become the bishop of St David's, and the other was to assert the independence of the Welsh church from Canterbury. In order to achieve his aims he even visited Rome on three separate occasions to fight his corner at the papal court itself. Despite his presentation to the pontiff of six of his books which, according to Gerald, the Pope kept at his bedside, he was, however, to receive no joy from Innocent III. The dice were too heavily weighted against Gerald for, politically, the stakes were too high. Innocent III, the ablest of the medieval popes, could hardly be expected to support his claims when such support would have alienated a king of England and his archbishop. Time only was to see the realisation of Gerald's dream, though in the early fifteenth century Owain Glyndŵr was to share his vision. It was not until 1920 that the church in Wales became entirely separate from Canterbury, and it was left to another ardent champion of Welsh aspirations, David Lloyd George, to complete what Gerald had begun.

It is undeniable that Gerald was very much a man of the world, a much-travelled cleric, and for about six or seven years his attendance at Court ensured that he was involved in a constant round of duties. Ireland, an island for which he had a particular affection, he visited on several occasions. In 1185 he went there as companion to Prince John, and he was to turn this visit to good account by collecting materials for two volumes on the history and geography of the country: the *Expugnatio Hibernica* (Conquest of Ireland) and the *Topographia Hibernica* (Topography of Ireland). These books were completed in his library at Llanddew, though it was at Oxford, another great centre of learning, that he was to publicise them by giving public readings and providing hospitality for his hearers at his own expense.

In 1188 Gerald embarked on another tour, on this occasion of his own native country of Wales. He accompanied Archbishop Baldwin around the peripheral areas of the peninsula in order to raise men and money to liberate Palestine from the clutches of the infidel Turk whose armies, in the previous year, under the leadership of Saladin, had captured Jerusalem. The itinerary began at Hereford and, after journeying for some five weeks around the coastal roads of Wales, the company finally arrived back at their original starting point. At New Radnor Gerald was so fired by a sermon preached by Baldwin that he was the first to step forward to proffer his services. He was never to join the crusade, for he got the papal legate to release him from his vow on the grounds of his poverty. The message preached must have been a powerful one, for at Hay so many men wanted to volunteer that wives and friends tried physically to restrain them from taking the cross. They only managed to escape their clutches by wriggling out of their garments and taking refuge with the archbishop in the castle. The following morning, the party left for Brecon, and Baldwin, having preached at Llanddew, decided to spend the night there. It was now that Gerald presented the primate with a copy of his work on the topography of Ireland. Baldwin received it graciously, and, according to Gerald, during the remainder of the itinerary he read, or heard read, parts of the book every day. He was to complete its perusal following his arrival back in England. This journey through Wales, though considerable areas remained untouched, provided Gerald with a rare opportunity for collecting material for tomes on Wales and predictably, in due course, there appeared the *Itinerarium Cambriae* (Itinerary of Wales) and his *Descriptio Cambriae* (Description of Wales).

The final years of his life were spent with his books at Lincoln, though he did again visit Ireland and embarked upon a spiritual pilgrimage to Rome. He died at Manorbier in March 1223 at the ripe old age of seventy-seven and, according to tradition, was laid to rest in the precincts of St David's.

Despite his undoubted talents, his vast scholarship, his indefatigable energy, his championship of what he considered to be the rightful status of St David's as a metropolitan see, he was not without his faults. Thus, he was vain, prejudiced, arrogant, conceited, credulous, quarrelsome, and extremely opinionated. But despite these considerable cracks in the mould, he was still a giant amongst Welsh medieval churchmen, and his books on Ireland and Wales have been, and will continue to be, rich veins of invaluable material to historians.

It is now time to leave the mouldering ruins within which Gerald once had a home and return to Brecon. After a good meal and a comfortable sleep, we shall be ready once again to embark on further forays into Brecon's past. This we will do on day 2.

NOTES

[1] Fox, A., 'Hill-slope forts and related earthworks in south-west England and South Wales', *Arch. Jnl.,* 1952.

[2] In memory of Candidus . . . son of . . .nus, trooper in the Vettonian Spanish Cavalry, Roman Citizen, set up by his heirs . . . Clemens and Domitius . . . he lived twenty years and served three. He lies here.

[3] It is as a builder that he is best known. He left his mark on the Cathedral Church of St David's which he considerably enlarged; at Swansea, he founded a hospital, and heightened the tower of the castle there. Furthermore, he repaired at least three churches, together with many of the episcopal manor houses, within the diocese.

Day 2: Llangorse and Tretower; Henry Vaughan

Refreshed after a good night's rest and a hearty breakfast, we are now prepared to meet the challenges of another day. On this occasion we will travel eastwards towards Llangorse and Tretower, but on the way, we shall take note of other sites and features of considerable historical interest.

We leave Brecon by the B4601 which takes us through an area of the town known as the Watton. Since the area is low-lying, and even today has willows growing in adjacent river meadows, the name probably derives from the Old English *wácor* meaning 'wicker' or 'willow'. The 'ton' element in the word is a later form of the Old English 'tún', an enclosure, homestead, village, or town.

In the Watton, and a few yards beyond the Trustee Savings Bank, which itself stands on the site of the county gaol, erected in 1690, is to be found a carpet warehouse. In the eighteenth century the 'New Inn' was located there, and behind the inn the 'Theatre Royal'. This playhouse was frequented regularly by the urban gentry of Brecon during their leisure hours, and it was gentry patronage, indeed, which enabled provincial theatres like the Royal to exist at all. The 'Theatre Royal' was established in 1787 by a resourceful Irishman by the name of John Boles Watson. He had played with Roger Kemble, the father of the immortal Sarah Siddons, and had inherited his circuit. Much to the discomfiture and annoyance of the 'genteel' element, especially the ladies, entry was effected through the inn itself. The 'New Inn' and the theatre were both owned by Andrew Maund, a local builder, and from his will it appears that he and Watson had entered into some form of partnership concerning the playhouse. The theatre was fitted up and decorated by Abbott, and plays and ballets were presented there. The productions included *Alexander the Great, The School For Scandal, The Heiress, Ella Rosenburg, All in the Wrong*, and *Don Juan* or *The Libertine Destroyed*. Watson and his son played on its boards; so did Andrew Cherry, the first manager of the new theatre at Swansea (1807), who had once been a leading actor at Drury Lane. It was the need to find fashionable audiences during the winter months that drove him to Brecon, where his company played before full houses.

Andrew Cherry.

Today, the 'Theatre Royal' is no more; the glory days are gone. A growing indifference to the theatre had gradually developed in the Victorian age. An increasing emphasis on outward respectability led serious-minded men and women to stay away, since theatres were regarded as the haunts of the frivolous and the feckless. Furthermore, it was clear that a certain degree of immorality was linked with performances, and the playhouses did attract prostitutes. Gentry patronage, so vital to the existence and survival of the theatre was, in many instances, withdrawn. Indeed, gentlemen who supported players came to be regarded as being either gay or eccentric. The Methodist Revival did not help either, as the leaders of that great awakening warned their followers that players were the Devil's own children. The problems of the theatre were further compounded by the insatiable demand for novelties, and even by the new fashion of dining late. Little theatres like the Royal closed their doors, and the buildings were put to other uses. It was a sad end to a glorious chapter.

Following this pause in our itinerary, we proceed along the B4601 passing on our left, a few hundred yards down the road, the barrack buildings. From Roman times Brecon has always maintained close links with the military. In the eighteenth century, troops had been accommodated at the 'Old Lion Inn' and, much to the consternation and alarm of many of the inhabitants, gunpowder had been stored in the town hall. In 1805 the justifiable fears of the inhabitants were somewhat allayed because the government now built a red-brick building for the storage of ammunition, powder, and arms in the Watton, along the road leading from Brecon to Abergavenny. It was a two-storey structure and, in 1813, the lower storey was equipped as an armoury, though, later, the armoury was converted into a barracks with accommodation for 270 men. It was from these barracks that in the 1830s soldiers were dispatched to quell the Merthyr riots (1831), the Chartist riots at Llanidloes and Newport (1839), and the nocturnal activities of Rebecca and her 'daughters',[1] who were clandestinely engaged in the destruction of tollgates in south-west Wales, beginning with the gate at Efailwen in 1839.

Following in the wake of Lord Cardwell's army reforms, the barracks acquired an enhanced importance, since Brecon became the military centre for the counties of Brecknock, Radnor, Montgomery, and Monmouth. The town now became home to the South Wales Borderers, and it was a detachment of this regiment that gained eternal fame by resisting so bravely the Zulu warriors at Rorke's Drift in 1879. This engagement followed the disaster at Isandhlwana, when a combined British and native force of 1,300 men was massacred. Seven Victoria Crosses were awarded to members of the company in recognition of their outstanding valour.

Further along the road, just beyond County Garage on the right hand side, there is a much altered tollgate house. The tollgates—and Brecon was like a besieged town with five gates altogether—had come into existence through the initiative shown by local landowners of substance, who had established Turnpike Trusts. The trusts raised money initially by issuing bonds on which a fixed rate of interest, usually five per cent, was paid. Cash was also raised through the erection of gates along the roads at which tolls were collected.

The Chartist attack on Newport, 1839.

Rebecca and her Daughters attack a tollgate.

This revenue was used to build and maintain tollgate houses, pay tollgate keepers, and to maintain the roads in a reasonable state of repair. The first Brecon Turnpike Act was enacted in 1767; twenty years later, in 1787, another was passed. At the beginning of the nineteenth century, in 1809, a single trust was established for the whole county known as the Breconshire Turnpike Trust and the trustees, without exception, were men prominent in the life of the county. They had to be in possession of land to the annual value of £80, or own estates to the value of £2,000 over and above all debts.

At Brecon, because of the greater damage they could cause to the road surface, carts carrying lime with wheels less than six inches wide, paid 3*d*. This toll on lime was particularly resented by the farmers, as the lime was extensively used as a fertilizer. However, Breconshire, with one exception, was spared the attentions of Rebecca. It was on a summer night in 1844 that Rebecca made her sole appearance in the county, when she and her daughters destroyed the gate at Tair-derwen, two miles outside Brecon on the road to Builth. One explanation for Rebecca's absence may be found in the fact that Brecon farmers were exempt from toll at any of the gates raised between the town and the kilns at Dorlan Goch.

Behind the tollgate house, and running parallel with the road, is to be found the Brecon and Abergavenny canal, and the act of Parliament which gave birth to this artificial waterway was passed in March 1793. The canal company, most of whose proprietors were local people, held its first meeting in the 'Golden Lion' inn in Brecon on 16 May 1793. The initiative sprang from the very laudable desire to reduce the price of coal and lime at Brecon. To cover the costs of construction—canals did not come cheaply —the company was empowered by the act to raise £100,000 through the sale of shares, the value of which was not to exceed £100, and no person could hold more than fifty. The proprietors could raise a further £50,000 among themselves, if it was deemed necessary. The act also empowered the company to build tramroads up to eight miles from the canal, and if the company did not wish to do so, then colliery owners were given the authority.

A scene on the Brecon to Abergavenny Canal.

The building of the canal from Gilwern to Brecon was started in 1797, and by November it had reached Llangynidr, eight and a half miles away. This was an extraordinary rate of progress especially when it is considered that the canal was four and a half feet deep and nine feet wide. Among the contractors were those who were clearly Welsh, men like Edward Price of Llangynidr (who also worked on the Neath canal), Thomas and Evan Lloyd of Llanelly (Brecs.), Joseph Needham of Crickhowell, and Thomas Parry of Llangattock; others, like William Macdonald and Thomas Dunn, came from England, the former from Matlock in Derbyshire, and the latter from Gloucester. There was only one contractor who was quite obviously Irish and that was Patrick Murphy.

Llangynidr having been reached, the remaining ten miles from there through Tal-y-bont to Brecon were completed by 1 December 1800, and on 24 December the first boatload of coal was brought to Brecon from the Gelli-Felen colliery, sunk on land belonging to the Duke of Beaufort and operated by one Edward Kendall. It would appear that the canal reduced the price of coal at Brecon from about 14*d.* per cwt. to 9*d.*, thus fulfilling the expectations of its founders.

In March 1802 it was decided to extend the canal southwards from Gilwern to Llanfoist, the site of the Abergavenny wharf, and by 14 January 1805 this stretch was completed. Though it was never originally envisaged that the Brecon to Abergavenny canal should join the Monmouthshire canal, in 1812 the junction was made, and the union had the effect of increasing considerably the annual revenue of the Brecon company. The increased flow of traffic on the canal meant that additional wharves had to be built at Brecon and Gilwern, and J. Wood's 'Plan of Brecknock', 1834, shows four wharves there.

Most of the labourers or navvies were probably Irish as they were prepared to work at relatively cheap rates. However, there is some circumstantial evidence which suggests that a few of the labourers, at least, were recruited from the local agricultural population. Perhaps it is no coincidence that Sir Charles Morgan of Tredegar Park, member of Parliament for the borough of Brecon, and a proprietor of the Brecon to Abergavenny canal, was one of the leading promoters of a bill in Parliament to 'restrain the employment of labourers (on canal cutting) in the time of the corn harvest', and, when it failed, he declared that he 'despaired of getting in the corn'. Furthermore, three of the four navigators identified in the 1841 census were Welsh—William Powell, Hugh Jones, and James Davies.[2]

Direct trading on the canal soon became the province of the Brecon Boat Company, first mentioned in 1796. It was an independent company even though it was largely owned by canal shareholders. To maintain a constant supply of coal at Brecon, the Boat Company leased mines and, in the hey-day of the trade, sixteen boats, each carrying twenty-one tons, could be seen conveying the coal along the canal. These barges were drawn by horses, and the tow-paths are still extensively used by hikers. The Boat Company also owned limestone quarries, since lime, as well as coal, was in great demand. Together with coal and lime, agricultural products, iron, and building materials traversed the tranquil waters of the canal.

In the nineteenth century the construction of railways dealt a mortal blow to the Brecon canal. Steam finally arrived at Brecon in

1863, and on 1 May, the Brecon to Merthyr line was opened. Others followed in quick succession, and the canal was doomed. The Brecon Boat Company was the first to throw in the towel when, in 1865, it stopped trading. In the same year the Brecon and Abergavenny Company followed suit by offering itself for sale to the Monmouthshire Company. By the turn of the century, only one boat, the market boat from Newport, travelled the entire length of the canal, and in February 1933 the last toll was collected at Llanfrynach. Canals, like the Brecon and Abergavenny, had enriched and diversified the social and economic fabric of Wales, and when they ceased to exist as vital arteries of industry and commerce, a whole way of life inextricably linked with them disappeared as well. Today, the canal is mainly used by pleasure boats and barges.

We now take our leave of the canal and follow the B4601 as far as the Brynich roundabout where we join the A40. We travel along this road for about two miles before turning left at the 'Old Ford' for Pennorth and Llangorse Lake.

Llangorse Lake

Llangorse Lake or Llyn Syfaddan[3] is a beautiful sheet of water some two miles in length and one mile in width, with a total circumference of about five miles. The average depth of the lake is from nine to twelve feet, though in its deepest parts it is considerably more than that. Indeed, according to John Leland, it was some three fathoms deep in places. Formed by glacial action, it is the largest natural lake in south Wales. Man has been associated with it from prehistoric times and in the crannog, an inhabited artificial island on the north side of the lake, we have a legacy of early Iron Age Man.[4] When the Celts built the camp at Pen-y-Crug, the crannog at Llangorse, in all probability, was already occupied.

The crannog was first discovered by the Rev. E. N. Dumbleton, and in a paper read to the Cambrian Archaeological Association in 1870, he described his discovery in these terms: 'Within a bow-shot of the flat meadows on the north side (of the lake) there is an island that would appear but little above water, were it not for some small trees and brushwood that have fastened upon it . . . Sailing by

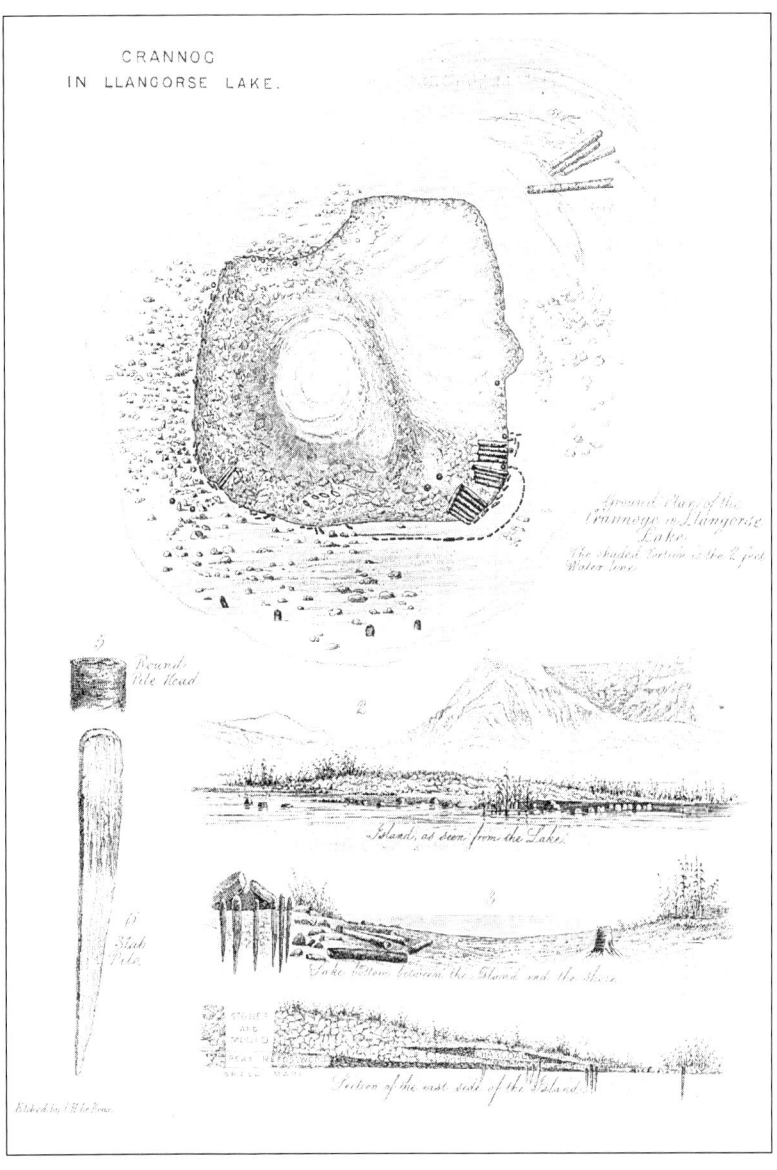

Crannog in Llangorse Lake.

31

the island one day in 1867, I observed that the stones which stood out on the south and east sides were strangely new-looking, and most unlike the water-worn and rounded fragments that on the main shore have been exposed to the action of the waves; neither did there seem to be any rock basis at all. It was, in fact, nothing less than a huge heap of stones thrown into the water three or four feet in depth. Was this the key, I thought, to the old tradition of a city in the lake? In the summer of last year, my brother, then living in the neighbourhood, first discovered a row of piles or slabs, some standing a few inches above water, for the lake was very low . . . The island, as now above water, measures 90 yards in circumference, its form being that of a square with the corners rounded off. The highest part is nearly in the centre, and is five feet above the water level. I must now speak of the piles. These are of two sorts, the most obvious being at the margin or within a few feet of it. Like the stones, they are most numerous where the action of the storm would be most felt, and upon the shallow side they disappear entirely. They have been disposed in segments of circles, the stones being heaped inside them, and thus saved from being torn away by the waves. These piles are of cleft oak, and have been pointed, as it seems, by cuts from a metal adze. We have counted about sixty. They have been driven tightly into the shell marl to the depth of four feet. There are also other piles, of which I shall have to speak again, which are round, generally of soft wood, and are found outside the present edge of the island. Several are in water two feet deep, and are driven into the marl only twelve or eighteen inches . . . We made several perpendicular openings, and these invariably led us down to the shell marl, showing first a stratum of large, loose stones, with vegetable mould and sand; next (about 18 inches above the marl), peat, black and compact; and beneath this the remains of reeds and small wood. This faggot-like wood presented itself abundantly . . . the object of it being, of course, to save the stones from sinking.'

From this account it becomes clear how these lake dwellings were constructed. Wooden piles were driven into the marl to a depth of about six feet and projecting from three to six feet above the water. A platform was then constructed on these piles, on which circular huts were built. The finds on the site have included teeth and bone fragments, and shards of pottery. On analysis, the bones turned out to be those of the horse, pig, ox, wild boar, and red deer.

In September 1925, about two hundred yards away from the crannog, a certain Tom Jenkins discovered a dug-out canoe. It was made from the trunk of a single oak tree, and was fifteen feet three inches in length. The canoe was two feet wide amidships with parallel sides, and these sides were about three inches thick. The internal depth of the boat was twelve inches. In the solid stern-end a seat had been cut, presumably for the steersman. From the construction of the boat it is quite apparent that its builders knew about the use of metal, either bronze or iron.

Llangorse dug-out canoe. (courtesy of Brecknock Museum)

Such canoes have often been found near crannogs, and they are certainly not uncommon in these islands. More than fifty have been discovered in Ireland and seventy in Scotland. However, not all dug-out canoes are of great antiquity. Such canoes were used in the Middle Ages and, in Westmorland, as late as the nineteenth century. They could be used for fishing, and were an obvious method, also, of crossing lakes. Radio-carbon testing has shown that the canoe found in Llangorse dates back to 500 A.D., to the period immediately following the departure of the Roman legions.

The lake is first mentioned in a charter of *c.* 720 A.D. By its terms, Awst, King of Brecknock, as an act of atonement, granted to Euddogwy, an early bishop of Llandaff, 'Lann Cors . . . with its fish and its fishery for eels'. Two hundred years later, the church at Llangorse was the scene of an important meeting between the ruler of Brycheiniog and Bishop Libiau of Llandaff. These early references point to two significant influences in the area in the post-Roman period: Irish settlement, and the introduction of Christianity.

After the departure of the legions, the Irish had been pushing into Wales from the west and Brychan, who gave his name to the Kingdom of Brycheiniog, was half-Irish. His mother, Marchell, was the daughter of Tewdrig, ruler of Garthmadryn; his father, on the other hand, was Anlach, son of Coronac, an Irish prince. Indicative, also, of Irish influences at Llangorse was the crannog, probably an Irish-type lake dwelling, and the only one of its kind found in Wales.

The other influence at work was Christianity. During the period of Roman occupation, it is doubtful whether there were any Christians in Brecknock. Following the departure of the Romans, Celtic saints, making use of the roads left by them, spread Christianity over the length and breadth of Wales, and churches dedicated to them dot the landscapes. Members of royal households, even, adopted the faith, and Brychan was reputed to have begotten a numerous progeny of twenty-four saintly daughters. The grant of fishing rights on Llangorse lake to the church, and the reputation enjoyed by the church there, are indicative of how strongly Christianity had become implanted in the area.

But the charter of 720 A.D. also focuses attention on the

importance of Llangorse lake as a source of food. From the time that man first trod its banks, the lake has been fished heavily. Even as late as the fifteenth century, widows and unmarried daughters from the suburb of Llanfaes at Brecon were attempting to eke out a precarious living by fishing with nets in Llangorse lake. It was the food resource provided by the lake that accounted for the fact that two of the three cantrefs of the old kingdom of Brycheiniog, Cantref Mawr and Cantref Talgarth, had a common boundary which ran through its centre.[5] And the parishes of Llangorse and Llangasty are similarly divided by an imaginary line running through the centre of the lake.

The importance of the lake economically was further exemplified when Bernard de Newmarch, the Norman conqueror of Brecknock, granted to his new foundation, the priory church of St John the Evangelist, extensive rights and properties there. Included in these grants was the right of advowson to Llangorse church and fishing rights on the lake. The black monks of Brecon priory were allowed to fish there daily in Advent and Lent, and on three days a week at other times.

The earliest map of the lake was drawn in 1584. It is a fairly accurate representation of the lake, and it contains features which again illustrate the importance of the lake in the local economy. Fishing is represented by two boats—little attention has been paid to scale—which bear a striking resemblance to the dug-out canoe, and at two fields' distance from the outlet there are two devices which are clearly eel pots or traps. Where the river Llynfi enters the lake there is a mill for the grinding of corn. A survey of the lake made towards the middle of the seventeenth century confirms its economic importance. The lake was described as 'well stored with eels, pikes and perch . . . and . . . under a certain bridge . . . are two weirs commonly called the King's weirs . . . at which said weirs are good store of eels taken in pots . . .' The surveyors estimated that fishing in the lake, and at the weirs, was worth £20 a year.

In a lease dated 1529 the isolation and seclusion of the lake became desirable features. A lessee there of the prior of the Benedictine house at Brecon was enjoined by the terms of his lease to 'honestly furnish the cross-chamber, that when the Prior or his

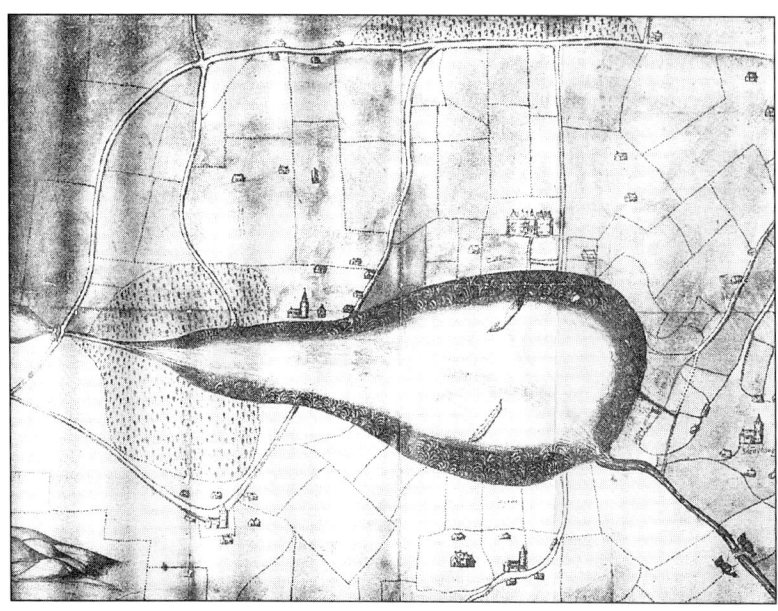

Llangorse, 1584.

successors, for fear of death, or other causes necessary, (wishes) then to have his chamber there . . .' The prior may well have had some premonition of impending doom for, a little later, between 1536-40, the monasteries were subject of a great act of nationalisation. Their lands were secularised and transferred, in the first instance, to the King, who then disposed of them by sale or lease to the gentry. In the event, priors and abbots were pensioned off. But in 1529 the prior at Brecon may have had every cause to make contingency arrangements for his own safety, as his fate at the hands of an imperious monarch such as Henry VIII was then uncertain. Indeed, the Welsh bards were to speak of *Llid y brenin yn lladd,* 'the anger of the King which is death'.

An early visitor to the lake was Gerald, and he was the first to set down his impressions in writing. He spoke of 'the famous lake of Brecknock (which) supplied the country with pike, perch, excellent trout, tench and eels'. He further observed that during the winter, when the lake was frozen over, it emitted a terrible moaning sound. This, he explained, was caused by the cracking of the ice, and the

36

sudden eruption of trapped pockets of air through vents indiscernible to the naked eye. This was a phenomenon also commented upon by John Leland, another great traveller, in the 1530s: 'After that it is frozen, and with thaw begins to break, it makes such a noise that a man would think it a thunder'.

Legends have always been inextricably linked with lakes. Tales of sunken cities figure very prominently in this mythology, engaging the attention of visitors and writers; and so it is with Llangorse. In 1804 the Rev. J. Evans reported that 'The country people say and believe that a city once stood there; but by a judgment of heaven for the sins of its inhabitants, it sunk into the earth, and water rose in the place'. This story was not unknown to the credulous Gerald, 600 years earlier, for he averred that 'it (the city) is sometimes seen by the inhabitants covered and adorned with buildings, pastures, gardens and orchards'. Again, events of a miraculous nature are associated with lakes. Gerald relates the tale of the birds of Llangorse which, while refusing to obey the command of Milo, the Norman lord of Brecknock, to sing for him, readily did so when commanded by the natural prince of the country, Gruffydd, the son of Rhys ap Tewdwr. They beat the water with their wings and cried aloud to proclaim him. In addition to the tale of the singing birds, Gerald also observed that even in his day, the waters of the lake had been seen to turn green or red, though not completely, as 'if blood flowed partially through certain veins and small channels'.

The flow of visitors to the lake was greatly increased in the nineteenth century by the arrival of the railway, which made the area far more accessible to tourists. The station at Tal-y-llyn was, after all, located within a mile of the lake. Guide books were published to advertise the attractions of the lake, and one described Llangorse as well stocked with fish 'with a fishing house close to the water, with accommodation for four visitors, at a charge for board and lodging of 7s. per day . . . There is also some excellent shooting in the way of wild fowl'. The railway has long since disappeared (courtesy of Dr Beeching), but the invention of the internal combustion engine has more than helped to plug the gap, since people arrive now in ever increasing numbers by car and coach. The fishermen are still in evidence, but they have to compete with power boats and water-skiers, and the peaceful serenity which once prevailed there is now interrupted by the roar of powerful engines. I shudder to think what Gerald would have thought of it all.

We now take our leave of Llangorse lake and proceed along the B4560 to Bwlch, where we link up with the A40. About two miles further along this road we turn left, and follow a narrow lane which leads us to Tretower Castle and Court.

Tretower Castle and Court

Tretower Court and Castle.   (courtesy of Cadw)

Tretower Castle

Over the centuries there were four principal phases in the development of the castle: first, in the early twelfth century, there was the motte and bailey fortification; secondly, in the mid-twelfth century, a stone shell keep was built which replaced the earlier timber defences; thirdly, in the succeeding century, a great circular tower was constructed, and the castle bailey was encompassed by stone walls; and finally, there was the abandonment of the castle as a place of residence, a change which may well have taken place by the fourteenth century.

Following the defeat of the local ruler, Bleddyn ap Maenarch and his overlord and brother-in-law, Rhys ap Tewdwr, at Battle in 1093, Bernard de Newmarch, the Norman conqueror of Brecknock, in 1100 conferred the Welsh commote of Ystrad Yw Uchaf on one of his followers, Sir Miles Picard. These knights' fees were granted on condition that certain services were rendered to the lord, and foremost among these obligations was the performing of military service for forty days annually and castle guard. It was in this manner that the lord provided for the defence of his castle and lordship.

Picard, to provide for his own safety, and to rivet his control firmly over his little domain, embarked immediately upon the construction of a castle. When selecting a suitable spot, he chose to ignore the site of a Roman fort nearby at Pen-y-gaer, and also the old Welsh settlement at Llanfihangel Cwmdu, two miles up the Rhiangoll. Instead, he built his castle in the main valley of the Usk at a point that enabled him to control effectively the junction of two major roads. The original fortification which he built was of earth and timber, and this motte and bailey castle could be erected very quickly, a great advantage in a period of conquest when he was surrounded by hostile Welsh. The mound or motte, which was surmounted by a wooden palisade, was quite small, since it was only about eighty or ninety feet in diameter. This motte was surrounded by a ditch thirty feet wide and revetted with a rough wall of stone. The revetment was necessary to stabilise the soil, as the ditch was filled with water brought from the Rhiangoll. The bailey or courtyard was roughly triangular in shape, and the defences would again have consisted of wooden palisades crowning earth banks. This kind of fortification, from the very nature of its construction, was obviously vulnerable to fire, and it was to offset this danger that rebuilding took place in the following century.

A view of Tretower Castle from the south.

It was towards the middle of the twelfth century that the wooden palisade on the motte was replaced by a stone wall, probably by Roger Picard or his son John. A shell[6] keep, almost circular in shape, was constructed with a contemporary gatehouse to the east. The hall and solar (private living quarters), an L-shaped block, were erected within this keep to the south-west. A kitchen, at a lower level, then occupied the space between the hall and the outer wall. The work is a fine example of Romanesque architecture, and ranks among the best surviving in Wales from this period.

In the first half of the thirteenth century Tretower Castle was modernised by another Roger Picard. An imposing circular tower was built on the centre of the motte and within the earlier shell keep. To provide room for this new feature the L-shaped block forming the hall and solar was removed, and the inner walls demolished. The round keep had been developed in France, and marcher lords campaigning there under King John (1199-1216) had observed it with interest. On their return they brought the idea back with them, and round keeps were established by William Marshall at Chepstow and Pembroke, and by Hubert de Burgh at Skenfrith. The lesser lights among the nobility emulated them, and included in their ranks were the Picards at Tretower.

The Tretower circular keep soars high above the shell keep, and was designed to give the garrison a clear field of fire over the outer parapet. It comprises three storeys together with a basement. Communication between this new tower and the curtain wall was provided by means of a bridge crossing from the west side of the former curtain wall-walk. Each storey consisted of a single room provided with fireplace and windows set in deep embrasures. It is clearly evident that the new structure was intended as a place of residence, however cold and uncomfortable it might be. At the same time, the bailey, which stood where the farm is located today, was surrounded by a stone curtain wall with circular towers at the angles, and substantial portions of this wall still remain. The strengthening of the bailey had become necessary because of the dynastic ambitions of Llywelyn ap Iorwerth or Llywelyn Fawr (1173-1240), prince of Gwynedd. In 1233 he had entered Brecknock, destroying and ravaging castles, towns, and countryside. It was during the time of Roger's son, another Roger (the Younger), that the great uprising under Llywelyn Fawr's grandson, Llywelyn ap Gruffydd (Llywelyn ein llyw olaf)[7] took place, culminating in Llywelyn's death at Cilmery, near Builth, in 1282. A report dispatched to Edward I in 1263 by Peter de Montfort indicated that the Welsh in the area had flocked to Llywelyn's standard, and that he controlled the country to within a few miles of Abergavenny.[8] The letter further suggested that Tretower and the other fortresses in the district had fallen to the Welsh prince. However, this might not have been the case, for it is known that Roger Picard, together with several other local lords, had taken an oath of homage and fealty to Llywelyn. It is possible, therefore, that Roger had been allowed to remain in possession of Tretower.

The family now decided to abandon the castle as a residence, and a new house was built two hundred yards to the south-east. This building, though it has been subjected to considerable change, is the northern part of Tretower Court. The transition was made from castle to domestic residence, from the cramped, confined conditions of the former to the relative comfort of the latter. It was a change that reflected an improvement in the political background, where a situation of endemic warfare and defence in the early

Middle Ages had been replaced in the fourteenth century by more peaceful conditions and greater stability.

However, even though the family had moved out, the castle was not allowed immediately to fall into decay. It remained a fortress capable of being used in times of war and in 1403, during the revolt of Owain Glyndŵr, Sir James Berkeley, who had inherited Tretower through marriage to an heiress, was ordered to furnish and garrison the castle and hold it for the King. Though the castle does not appear to have been put to any military use after this, a sketch made at the beginning of the sixteenth century shows the defences intact, with the great tower still rising high above the shell keep, and other towers standing at the angles of the bailey.

Tretower Court

The original hall-type manor house was of modest proportions, indicative of the fact that the new owners, the Bluets, had their principal residence at Raglan. For them, the small house at Tretower would have served as the administrative centre of the manor, and could also have been used by them as a residence when a visit was made. The last of the Picards, John, had died without male heirs in 1305, and it was his heiress, Anicia, who brought Tretower to her husband, Ralph Bluet. During succeeding centuries Tretower Court developed according to the needs and tastes of successive owners. As it now stands, the house consists of two accommodation ranges, and two wall-walks encompassing a large central courtyard. The north range is essentially fourteenth century, the west range fifteenth century, and the gate-house and wall-walks in the south and east are late fifteenth-century additions.

The early country house, which is the present north range, was stone-built to the roof. It consisted of a central ground floor hall open to the rafters with, on the upper floor, and at the west end, a private living room and bedchamber, and in the east, also on the upper floor, and beyond the hall, a separate apartment. In the early fifteenth century, during the troubles occasioned by the uprising of Owain Glyndŵr (1400-15), the house appears to have been gutted by his followers.

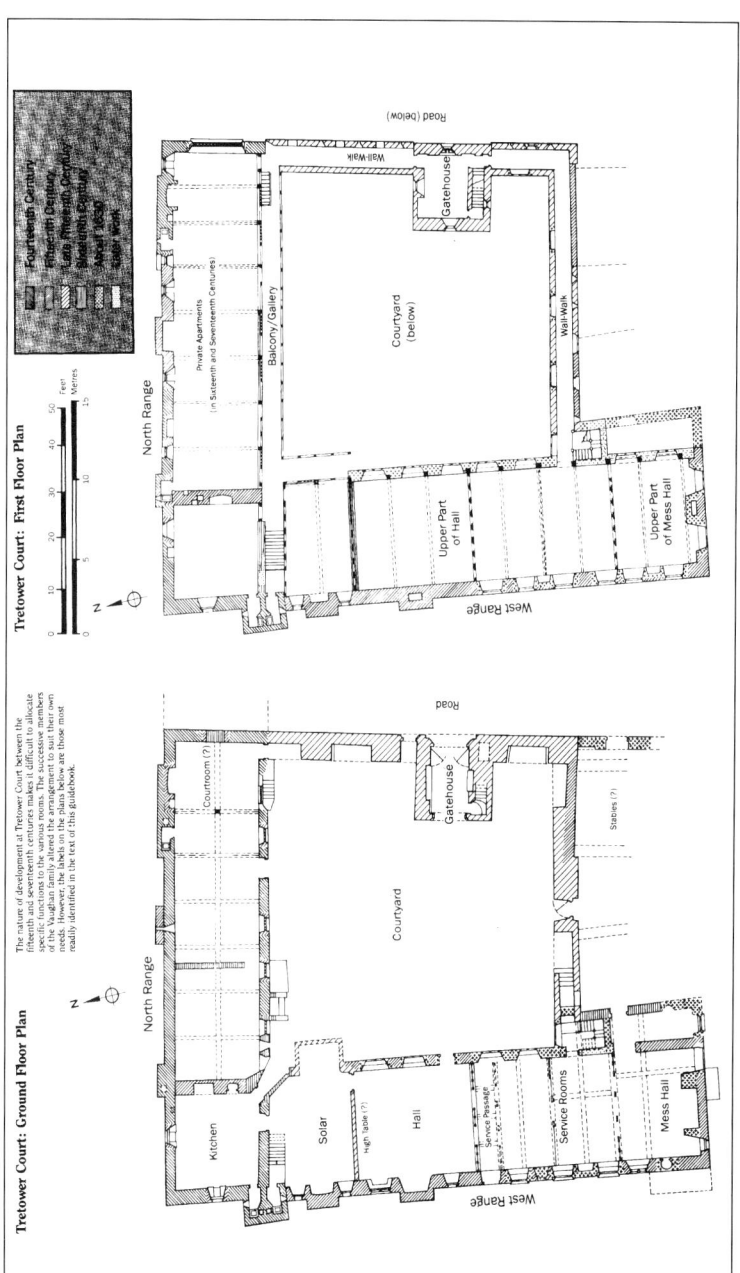

Tretower Court: Ground Floor Plan

The nature of development at Tretower Court between the fifteenth and seventeenth centuries makes it difficult to allocate specific functions to the various rooms. The successive members of the Vaughan family altered the arrangements to suit their own needs. However, the labels on the plans below are those most readily identified in the text of this guidebook.

North Range

Kitchen
Solar
High Table (?)
Hall
Service Passage
Service Rooms
Mess Hall
West Range
Courtroom (?)
Gatehouse
Stables (?)
Courtyard
Road

Tretower Court: First Floor Plan

Feet
Metres

North Range

Private Apartments (in Sixteenth and Seventeenth Centuries)
Balcony/Gallery
Upper Part of Hall
Upper Part of Mess Hall
West Range
Courtyard (below)
Wall-Walk
Gatehouse
Wall-Walk
Road (below)

Fourteenth Century
Fifteenth Century
Late Fifteenth Century
Sixteenth Century
About 1630
Later Work

Tretower Court: ground-floor plan; first-floor plan.

(courtesy of Cadw)

Towards the middle of the fifteenth century the house came into the possession of the Vaughans. Roger Vaughan was given Tretower by his half-brother, Sir William Herbert, who also lavished on him grants of property in Brecknock and Glamorgan, which made Vaughan the richest commoner in the country. As a monument to his increasing wealth, prominence, and importance, Roger embarked upon an extensive programme of modernisation and new building. He converted the north range into a two-storey structure, and the south wall was replaced with a half-timbered front and a projecting balcony. While the upper floor was laid out in private apartments, the lower storey was used for storage with a kitchen at the west end. He also doubled the extent of his accommodation by adding a west wing, at the south end of which there was a separate mess hall for his retainers or men-at-arms. At this time, a bodyguard was indispensable for a man of his social standing.

At the close of the century, possibly about 1480, Roger's son, Sir Thomas Vaughan, continued the developments which his father had initiated. It was Sir Thomas Vaughan who added the battlemented wall-walk and gatehouse, thus enclosing the courtyard on the east and south sides which hitherto had been open. These additions echoed the defensive idea, and in the gatehouse there was an element which, clearly, was an offshoot of the tower. This development at Tretower Court was far removed from the style of the majority of gentry houses of the period which were completely undefended. It can be explained, possibly, on two grounds: pure ornamentation— an architectural folly—or else a miscalculation of the course of political developments in the late fifteenth century; an expectation that the unrest of the century was going to end in anarchy. This did not happen, for after the battle of Bosworth, 22 August 1485, the helm was in the iron grasp of the Tudors. Together with these additions, Sir Thomas also altered the hall and solar in the west range. It was this Sir Thomas Vaughan and his brothers, all ardent Yorkists, who helped to frustrate the Duke of Buckingham's plot in 1483 to overthrow Richard III and place Henry Tudor on the English throne. During the duke's absence from his lordship to foment rebellion, they dealt his cause a severe blow by capturing and plundering his base at Brecon castle.

Tretower remained in the hands of the Vaughans until 1783. It was then sold and became a farm. The seventeenth-century living rooms at the end of the west range remained occupied, but the other buildings were adapted for use as barns and sheds. After passing through other hands when the structure was neglected, it was finally bought by the Brecknock Society with financial help from the Pilgrim Trust. In 1930 it was transferred to the Commissioners of Works for proper repair and maintenance. Today Tretower Castle and Court are the responsibility of *Cadw*: Welsh Historic Monuments.

Perhaps the most eminent member of the Vaughan family was Henry Vaughan, the Silurist (1621-95), who lies buried in Llansantffraed. He was the son of Thomas Vaughan, a country gentleman of modest means[9] and Denise, the daughter and heiress of David Morgan of Newton. Tretower Court, set in the shadow of the Black Mountains, retains an interest as the only surviving house intimately associated with him. He, and his twin brother, Thomas, were both raised in the neighbourhood, and became pupils of the Rev. Matthew Herbert, rector of the neighbouring church of Llangattock. Both boys became poets and writers of some distinction and Henry's works, religious and secular, deservedly place him as one of the chief Anglican sacred poets of the seventeenth century. The Silurist, undoubtedly, was inspired by the beauty and tranquillity of the Usk valley, and a mystical rapture pervades many of his poems:

> But, Isca,[10] whensoe'er those shades I see,
> And thy lov'd arbours must no more know me,
> When I am laid to rest hard by thy streams,
> And my sun sets where first it sprang in beams,
> I'll leave behind me such a large, kind light,
> As shall redeem thee from oblivious night.

Other powerful influences in his life were those provided by the religious poems of George Herbert and his love of church and Bible.

When he was seventeen, he proceeded to Jesus College, Oxford, founded in 1571 by a Brecon man, Dr Hugh Price. Destined by his father for the law, after two years at Oxford, Vaughan moved to the

Inns of Court, London. Following a legal apprenticeship there, interrupted by the outbreak of the English Civil War in 1642, he returned to his native heath, and was appointed clerk to Sir Marmaduke Lloyd, Chief Justice of the Brecon Circuit of the Court of Great Sessions. It is quite possible that at this time he resided in Brecon town, for it was in the Priory Groves that he met the lady who was to become his beloved wife and the mother of four of his eight children. She was Catherine Wise,[11] a member of a Worcestershire family and related to Sir Herbert Price of Priory House. Vaughan and Colonel Price were to fight for the Royalists in the English Civil Wars, and Vaughan's allegiance was determined by his love of monarchy and church, institutions which he held to be sacred. He fought at Rowton Heath about two miles to the southeast of Chester when a close friend fell in the heat of the battle, an experience which he never forgot. He compared his death to the fall of 'a well-built elm or stately cedar on some river's flow'ry brow'. Following the final defeat of the King, Henry Vaughan sheathed his sword and picked up the pen, and his major works were all written during the next seven years, between 1648 and 1655. Thereafter he appears to have abandoned authorship. His books had not received much popular acclaim, and there were also the pressing demands of his new profession, medicine. Earlier, about 1650, he had experienced conversion to a religious life, and this change was brought about by the operation of factors such as the influence of the poet George Herbert, the death of a dearly loved brother, William, his rediscovery of the Bible as he, himself, lay close to death during a serious illness, the loss of his wife, Catherine, and the distress caused by the 'distempered' times. Little is known about the forty years of his life stretching from 1655 to 1695. It is possible that he had begun practising medicine, 'with good success', at Llansantffraed and the neighbouring districts during the Commonwealth period, but when or how he became a doctor is still shrouded in darkness. In later life he was troubled by ill-health and family dissensions, and lawsuits over property are recorded. As an old man, the 'Swan of Usk' (*Olor Iscanus*) left Newton to live in a cottage attached to the east side of Tretower house. Regrettably, the cottage has long since been pulled down.

His name will always be perpetuated in his poetic and prose works. However, his apparent skill as a doctor has now earned him a more tangible memorial, for when the new Brecon surgery was opened in 1994 in Llanfaes, just beyond the Usk bridge, it was resolved to name it after him.

We will now abandon Tretower Castle and Court to the ghosts of the past, and rejoin the A40 for our return journey to Brecon. There we will refresh and prepare ourselves for yet another day of discovery.

NOTES

[1] The rioters were men who dressed in women's clothing.

[2] I am grateful to J. R. Norris for this information.

[3] The lake of the standing water or the lake at the bottom.

[4] The Early Iron Age covers a period of some 600 years, from about 500 B.C. onwards.

[5] The other was Cantref Selyf.

[6] The walls of a shell keep were not particularly thick, as an artificial earth mound would not have been able to sustain an enormous weight of masonry.

[7] Llywelyn our last ruler.

[8] 'Every man of Welsh speech of the lords . . . in short the whole Welshry down to the borders of the land of Abergavenny, has turned to Llywelyn, so that the frontier of the men of the said Llywelyn lies only a league and a half from Abergavenny'.

[9] According to an inventory of Thomas Vaughan's possessions taken at the time of his death in 1658, his goods were valued at just £5, a surprisingly low figure. However, the furniture and effects might well have represented what many of the poorer Welsh gentry possessed at the time. While there were many pewter vessels, there was no silver. Furthermore, the house in which he dwelt was unpretentious. On the ground floor it consisted of a hall, study, a large kitchen and buttery; the first floor comprised a small room over the porch, a substantial room over the kitchen, rooms over the study and hall, and a garret. Doubtless, there would also have been outhouses, or lean-to buildings, such as a wash-room, brewery and dairy.

[10] Usk.

[11] Following the death of Catherine, Henry Vaughan married her sister, Elizabeth.

Day 3: Elston's Garage, the Forge, Bronllys Castle and Cilmery; the Drovers

Today, with full tanks, let us travel in a northerly direction along the A470 to Builth Wells, and from there along the A483 to Cilmery, where Llywelyn ap Gruffydd, the last prince of Wales, was slain in 1282. On the way through the Struet to link up with the A470, we shall pass Elston's garage, the original home of electricity in Brecon; then, the forge on the banks of the Honddu where, surprisingly, iron was produced in the eighteenth century; afterwards, the tower at Bronllys where a Norman lord met with a violent end; and, finally, the hallowed spot at Cilmery. On the return journey we shall follow a scenic route over the Epynt mountain, and trace one of the roads used by the drovers in the hey-day of their activities.

The river Honddu which, for a short distance, runs parallel with the road, has not only provided sport for fishermen over the years; it has also been the source of energy for Brecon's industrial activity. It was the power provided by this rapidly-flowing river that was utilised by the flannel factory that once stood in the shadow of the Chapter House and Deanery,[1] and drove the turbines which enabled Harold Percival Elston to generate electricity at his garage located on its banks.

Harold Elston was not a native of the area. His parents had moved into Brecon from the West Country, and his father had found employment with Eastman, a butcher with a shop in the High Street. The father had soon set up on his own, and this business was located in premises opposite Woolworth's, now the Hideway Cafe. When his father died, Harold Elston left Brecon County School at the age of thirteen. However, he did not follow in his father's footsteps, for he chose to pursue a three-year engineering course with Messrs Archdales, Ballus, and Morecombe in Birmingham. On completion of this course, in 1908 he began a five-year apprenticeship at the Brecon and Merthyr Railway engineering works in Machen and Newport. He then returned to Brecon and, in 1913, when he was only twenty-one years of age, he established his own business.

Elston's Garage and brewery buildings.

This was a small garage at Pendre, next to the tollgate house, and near to the present entrance to the new housing estate at Maes-y-ffynnon. A bungalow was also built there by the family and named 'Burtlands', in honour of Burt Elston who had been killed in Palestine in 1917 during the First World War (1914-18). The butcher's business in the High Street, in the meantime, was carried on by Harold's mother, and his brother, Tom. The garage business prospered, and Harold Elston, in search of larger premises, moved to the site of the Old Mill in the Struet, where the garage still stands today.

In 1914, when hostilities began between Britain and Germany, Harold Elston was appointed war agricultural engineer, and was contracted by the Ministry to maintain tractors and machinery. He was also made the official oxy-acetylene welder to the Ministry for the whole of south Wales and Monmouthshire, and became involved, as well, in the manufacture of munitions. In 1916, he became the main Ford dealer in Breconshire, there being only four others in the whole of Wales at the time. His territory was to be considerably augmented in 1925 when the Ford Motor Company offered him the franchise in Radnorshire. It was in 1920 that he installed a hydro-electric plant on his premises to supply adjacent areas of Brecon with electricity. It was he who supplied 'The George Hotel', the licensee of which at the time was George Hargest;[2] houses and businesses in the Struet, the High Street, and Castle Street were also his customers. Among the businesses supplied were his brother Tom's butcher's shop in the High Street, and Stanton the Chemist at the top of Castle Street, the old Boot's. Cables were also run to Nythfa, the Cathedral, houses in St John's Road and North Road, and even to Pwll-y-Calch farm situated high up on Cradoc Road. By 1925 Harold Elston had two main cables running into the town, and was supplying thirty-three consumers.

Before the introduction of electrical power, the streets and larger premises of Brecon, such as substantial dwellings, schools, and theatres, had been lit by gas, which had been introduced into Brecon in 1822, though it was not until 1856 that the Brecon Gas Company was established. However, the municipal authority displayed a marked reluctance to introduce any scheme of electrification even though, as early as 1900, it had applied to the Board of Trade for permission to light by electricity and to lay underground cables. Thereafter, nothing was done. It was not until 1924 that the town council inaugurated a scheme for supplying electricity, and then it was in response to a growing clamour for the facility from the ratepayers, who had made repeated representations to the council.

Following these representations, the town council approached the Brecon Chamber of Trade to request it to contact its members to ascertain the nature of the demand amongst the business community. At a special meeting of the Chamber of Trade held in the Council Chamber on 11 December 1924, it was resolved to establish a committee with a remit to explore the matter. No time was wasted, for on 15 December Stanley E. Jenkins, the President of the Chamber of Trade, sent a circular letter to all members inviting their views. In it he declared that the cost of installation would be in the region of 25s. a light, and that after this initial outlay, the cost of the electricity consumed would approximate to that of gas for the same amount of light. He further emphasised that the scheme would only be practicable if all the business people of the town supported it. A half-hearted attitude could only be unhelpful. Enclosed with the letter was a list of the advantages which would accrue from the adoption of electricity. These were: cleanliness, which would reduce the cost of redecorating by half; convenience and economy, as it was easy to switch on and off; safety, for the risk of fire would be minimised; health, because the atmosphere of shops, offices, and living rooms would be 'less vitiated'; and finally, window dressing and display, where the advantages were so obvious as to need no further clarification.

Such a scheme of electrification, were it to be accepted by the town council, quite obviously would have had serious repercussions for Harold Elston's generating plant at his garage. So, naturally enough, on 10 June 1925, he wrote a letter of objection to the electricity commissioners in London. In this he made three representations: first, that the town council, though it had been approached on numerous occasions, had turned down requests for a municipal scheme on the grounds that it would not be profitable; secondly, he had progressively attempted to meet an obvious need by pushing out more feeders, and this development had involved him in considerable expense; and thirdly, a municipal scheme would be a very heavy burden on the rates, and he would have to pay his share even though he had his own private supply. Since he wanted the ratepayers to know the grounds for his objection, he invited the editor of the *County Times* to publish in full his letter to the commissioners.

As was to be expected, the Gas Company also voiced objections to the scheme for electrification, and this objection was reported in the *County Times* on 14 January 1926. However, despite the protests, Brecon Borough Council proceeded with its proposals for a town electricity supply which became known as the Brecon Electric Light Scheme. On 2 December 1926 the *County Times* reported that the Brecon Borough Council had decided to locate the municipal power station near the slaughter-house in Canal Road, and, on the evening of 1 January 1928, it was formally opened by the mayor, Councillor W. J. Bevan. Although the Brecon Electric Light Scheme Order had passed through both Houses of Parliament on 16 December 1926, it was not until 14 September 1927 that the town council met to appoint a Clerk of Works, who was to receive a salary of £250 per annum. Three applicants were short-listed for interview, and the successful applicant was Arthur Pluck, Chief Electrical Engineer of the Ogmore and Garw Urban District Council. Events were now moving fast, and on 2 February 1928 Messrs Coppages of Brecon were advertising a demonstration of cooking, washing, cleaning, and heating by electricity. Brecon Town Council did not remain the authorised provider of electricity for long, as in 1935 this franchise was purchased by the Shropshire, Worcestershire and Staffordshire Electric Power Company. The South Wales Electricity Board was eventually to become the supplier. Harold Elston, however, was not to be outdone. The spirit of private enterprise still burnt fiercely within him, and in 1926 he was advertising 'house wiring'. But it was not an even playing field; he was, after all, in competition with a powerful company and in 1936 he, also, had to follow the example of the Town Council and sell out to the S.W.S.

Together with being a pioneer in the provision of electricity, Harold Elston was also experimenting with, and promoting development in, the fields of radio and television. He designed three-, four-, and five-valve radio sets and, having obtained a licence from the B.B.C., he started production on two- and three-valve radios known as 'Elston-phones'. By 1931 he had made and sold over 3,500 of these. The first 'foreign' reception obtained by him was the Carpentier-Dempsey world heavyweight title fight from America, the signal being received by an aerial erected on Crug Hill. Television, also, received attention and, as early as 1931, he was receiving pictures from Alexandra Palace.

Harold Elston managed to combine successfully a busy business schedule with an active interest in local government. For many years he was a borough councillor, and was mayor of Brecon in 1930-1. But his involvement did not end there, for he was President of Brecon Chamber of Trade, chairman of the mid-Wales Section of the Motor Agents' Association, and chairman of the East Wales Division of the M.A.A. For his services to the motor industry, he was elected a Fellow of the Institute of the Motor Industry, and a Member of the Institute of British Engineers.

During the Second World War, 1939-45, as in the First, he played his part in the war effort by manufacturing component parts for torpedo nets for the Admiralty, and such was the demand for these that, until 1944, twenty-four hour shifts had to be worked.

On 26 October 1951 Harold Elston's business empire suffered a severe blow when the whole of the Struet was lit like a candle by the flames which totally destroyed his garage. In a matter of hours the labours of a lifetime were reduced to ashes. However, such were his resilience and determination that within eighteen months a new, and more up-to-date, garage had been both planned and erected.

Adjoining Harold Elston's garage was the Brecon Old Brewery which, at one time, was owned by a Llanfaes man, David Powell. Within the curtilage of the brewery there was also a 'pop' factory. Before the introduction of motor-powered vehicles, the beer was delivered by horse-drawn drays, and on the premises in the Struet there was stabling for horses. Since leisure hours were spent in the convivial atmosphere of inns—and in Brecon these abounded—beer was quaffed in great quantities, and the beer produced in the Struet was, apparently, of a particularly good quality. Indeed, following the arrival of the railway in Brecon, visitors were to be encouraged to visit the town by the attraction of Brecon's own ale, 'a prime ale, made of water, malt and hops, without the infusion of tobacco or any article of a deleterious nature'. During the Second World War the brewery closed its doors, but the louvre ventilator on the roof of the building can still be seen, and one can read on a board in front of the building, although the lettering is very faint, the words 'Brecon Brewery'. In 1988 the property was sold for development.

We now leave Elston's, and about a hundred yards further up the road, in the direction of Bronllys, there is a lane leading off to the left. This lane takes us to the site of the furnace on the banks of the Honddu which, during the eighteenth century, echoed, however faintly, the vast industrial activity taking place in the valleys of south Wales.

Since there were no iron deposits in Brecon, it might appear surprising, at first glance, that a furnace and forge should have been established there. After all, the great centre of the iron industry was the north-eastern rim of the south-Wales coalfield, an area exdending from Hirwaun in the west to Blaenavon in the east. This iron belt was roughly eighteen miles in length and one mile in width.

Brecon furnace, 1720.

The furnace and forge at the Groves in Brecon, and the forge at Pipton, on the banks of the Llynfi, were established by Benjamin Tanner, an ironmonger of Brecon, and Richard Wellington, a gentleman of Hay, as co-partners in 1720. The original lease of the land on the banks of the Honddu had been granted by Edward Jeffreys of the Priory, who wished to exploit the economic potential of his estate. The site was one that offered considerable advantages, since an old corn-mill had previously stood there, and a mill-pond and leet were ready to hand for conversion by the new lessees. Furthermore, in the Honddu, a river with a particularly strong current, there was enough water power to drive the huge bellows necessary to produce a strong blast of air, without which a sufficiently intense heat could not be produced to smelt the iron ore.

It was the rapid diminution of the timber resources in the valleys of south-east Wales that provided the stimulus to encourage iron production at Brecon. Even after Abraham Derby's revolutionary technique for smelting iron by coke or burnt steam coal had been developed at Coalbrookdale in the early eighteenth century, charcoal, until about 1750, was still the agent primarily employed for the smelting of iron in Wales. At Brecon and its environs there was an abundance of oak and other woods. But the all-devouring furnace could also be supplied from the coppice woods in Cwmdwr valley, beyond Llywel, and even by others as distant as those in the Wye valley, and across the Epynt mountain at Llangamarch and Llanwrtyd. The supply of charcoal being thus assured, the iron ore, and the limestone required for fluxing, were carried in sacks on the backs of horses and mules from Hirwaun, some eighteen miles away. A forge was later added to the Brecon furnace. The annual output of 400 tons of iron produced from the furnace also fed the forge at Pipton, and the iron was then taken to Hay, six miles from Pipton, and conveyed by barge down the Wye to Chepstow, and thence to Bristol to be disposed of by the merchants of that city. The transportation costs were heavy, and the price of iron was also high, probably exceeding £20 a ton. Iron production in the eighteenth century had become extremely profitable, even in a remote area like Brecon, because of the insatiable demand for the product provided by the recurring wars of the century, the building of iron bridges following the construction of Ironbridge in 1779, and machine-building for an ever-expanding textile industry.

In 1750, the Brecon furnace, together with the forge at Pipton, were bought by Thomas Daniels and Richard Reynold, iron merchants of Bristol, from Benjamin Tanner's son, William. They held the works for only three years before selling them for £400 to Thomas Maybery, who had previously been engaged in iron production at the Powick forge in Worcestershire. Maybery immediately transferred the works to his son, John, who, a little later, in 1757, erected a furnace at Hirwaun. For a while, John Maybery was in sole charge, but in 1760 he took his brother-in-law, John Wilkins, a Brecon banker, into partnership. The works then 'rapidly developed and became profitable'. Four years later, John

Maybery leased the Tredegar forge and, in 1777, in partnership with Wilkins, he also leased the ironworks at Machen. These developments had disastrous consequences for the Brecon works, and the roar of the bellows and the glow from the furnace were not to be heard or seen for much longer in the town. As pig-iron could be made far more cheaply at their forges in Hirwaun, production at Brecon was gradually abandoned, and by 1800 the furnace and forge were silent. The closure of the works could hardly have been a matter of regret for the worthy citizens of the ancient borough.

Bronllys Castle by Samuel and Nathaniel Buck.

We now rejoin the road leading to the A470 and, leaving the 'industrialised' suburb of the Struet behind us, proceed to Builth Wells. However, at Bronllys, let us take a slight detour and turn right on to the A479 Talgarth road. A few hundred yards along this road, to the left, on a slight eminence overlooking the river Llynfi, is located Bronllys[3] Castle.

The Norman Conqueror of Brecknock, Bernard de Newmarch, had pushed into the kingdom from Hereford via the Wye valley. He allotted Hay to William Revel, and a timber castle was built there. By 1088 Bernard had penetrated as far as Glasbury and here, instead of pursuing the course of the river northwards, he struck south along the Llynfi valley and took possession of Talgarth, the old Welsh capital of Brycheiniog. Bronllys was awarded to another of his faithful knights, one Richard fitz Pons, lord of Clifford. This policy of granting knights' fees to his followers was one pursued by Bernard over the whole of Brecknock, and these *conquistadores* then riveted their control over the countryside by building fortifications at strategic points. As was to be expected, the majority of these castles were erected in the lush valleys of the Wye and the Usk.

Richard fitz Pons, once in possession of his knight's fee, promptly built his castle at the confluence of the Dulais and Llynfi rivers. It consisted of a wooden motte built on an earthen mound over a rock outcrop and two baileys or courtyards: an inner courtyard which was triangular in shape, and an outer one beyond it. It is possible that the timber motte had been replaced by some kind of masonry structure in the twelfth century, because in 1175 Giraldus Cambrensis mentions a stone falling from the principal tower and fatally injuring Mahel, the lord of Brecknock. Mahel, 'a miserable covetous man', had been visiting Walter de Clifford when the castle accidentally caught fire. Gerald described Mahel as a cruel persecutor of David, the bishop of St David's. He attacked the bishop's possessions, lands, and vassals, and did so with such force that the bishop was compelled to flee into exile in England. When the grim reaper came to summon Mahel, the lord of Brecknock is reputed to have dispatched messengers to recall the bishop, and before he died, he did penance for his numerous acts of tyranny. In 1233 the castle was again ravaged by fire, but on this occasion it was no mischance; the arsonists were Welsh tribesmen led by Llywelyn ap Iorwerth.[4] In consequence of this onslaught, Walter de Clifford II built a circular tower in stone, with its foundations carried through to the rock; and the curtain walls and towers were also rebuilt of stone. These curtain walls were further protected on the north-west and south-east sides by a deep fosse or dry moat. In the fourteenth and fifteenth centuries the castle had a chequered history, and repeatedly changed hands. In 1450, Bedo Bronllys,[5] a celebrated bard of the age, lived there; and in 1508 it came into the possession of Edward Stafford, third Duke of Buckingham, the powerful marcher lord of Brecknock. In 1521, after a trial before a court of dubious legality, Buckingham was

Bronllys Castle.

59

attainted of treason and beheaded. A survey made of his estates following his death revealed that his castle at Bronllys had been abandoned and was already in a ruinous state. This state of dilapidation is confirmed by Samuel and Nathaniel Buck's engraving of 1741.

The most significant feature of the castle today is the thirteenth-century circular tower, which is over fifty feet in height. Originally, it must have been even higher, between sixty and seventy feet, and surmounted as well by a battlement now completely destroyed. The tower, which has a base diameter measuring thirty-seven feet, comprised a cellar and three floors. The entrance doorway was set high on the wall and could only have been approached by a ladder or moveable bridge. This doorway led into the hall, which was provided with two window embrasures. From one, a stair led downwards through the thickness of the wall to a vaulted cellar, which was used for storage. The steps only extended half-way down to the basement floor; the other half would have been negotiated by means of a portable ladder. A stair spiralled upwards from the other embrasure to a private chamber or solar, which had two embrasures with ogee-headed windows and a wall fireplace. Another stair then led to the more ruined top floor, which again was provided with a fireplace and three evenly spaced embrasures with seats. It was in the 1790s that the hall in the inner bailey, depicted in the Buck engraving,[6] was incorporated in a stable block of a new house. The curtain walls, even by 1741, had long since disappeared.

It is time now to abandon the tower to its solitary majesty and return to the A438 to continue our journey to Builth Wells. A short distance along the road to Three Cocks, we turn left and rejoin the A470 at Llyswen. Builth being reached, we link up with the A483 which leads us to Cilmery and the massive stone monolith which marks the spot where, according to tradition, Llywelyn ap Gruffydd's dream of establishing a united Wales, independent of England, ended so tragically in 1282.

Llywelyn was the second son of Gruffydd ap Llywelyn and grandson of Llywelyn ap Iorwerth. His career really took off in 1255 when, at Bryn Derwin, he defeated two of his brothers,

Owain and Dafydd, in battle, imprisoned them, and made himself the sole ruler of Gwynedd, a principality situated in north-west Wales. The imprisonment of Dafydd earned for Llywelyn his brother's lasting enmity.

Having established his power base, Llywelyn now embarked upon the realisation of his twin aspirations: a united Wales and independence from England. The obstacles strewn in his path were formidable, since Wales at the time was governed by independent Welsh rulers who were jealous of their powers, and mighty marcher lords, who had consolidated their hold over the territories which they had conquered by building castles. And across the border there was an implacable foe in the person of the English sovereign, who was determined to frustrate any attempts at creating a united Welsh principality.

However, though the path might be stony, there were a number of factors which favoured the Welsh prince as he sought to gain his objectives. First, his grandfather's achievements had created a degree of national fervour among the Welsh, and he had further pointed the way towards the establishment of a feudal state in Wales on the same lines as those that existed in contemporary England and France. The monastic orders, too, particularly the Cistercians, were loyal to the princes, and their houses were centres of Welsh learning, literature and culture. Moreover, the introduction of English laws, practices and customs in areas under royal and baronial control had alienated the local Welsh population and caused resentment among them. Finally, the struggle between Henry III and his barons had created a situation which Llywelyn could exploit to his own benefit.

But though it was the battle of Bryn Derwin that marked the appearance of Llywelyn on the national stage, he had, at an earlier period, given some indications of his intentions. In November 1250 he had entered into an agreement for mutual defence with Gruffydd Madog, and, in October 1251, he had been instrumental in securing a degree of co-operation between the rulers of Gwynedd and Maredudd ap Rhys and Rhys Fychan of Ystrad Tywi.

With his back door firmly closed behind him, Llywelyn, after 1255, embarked upon an expansionist policy. Meirionydd became

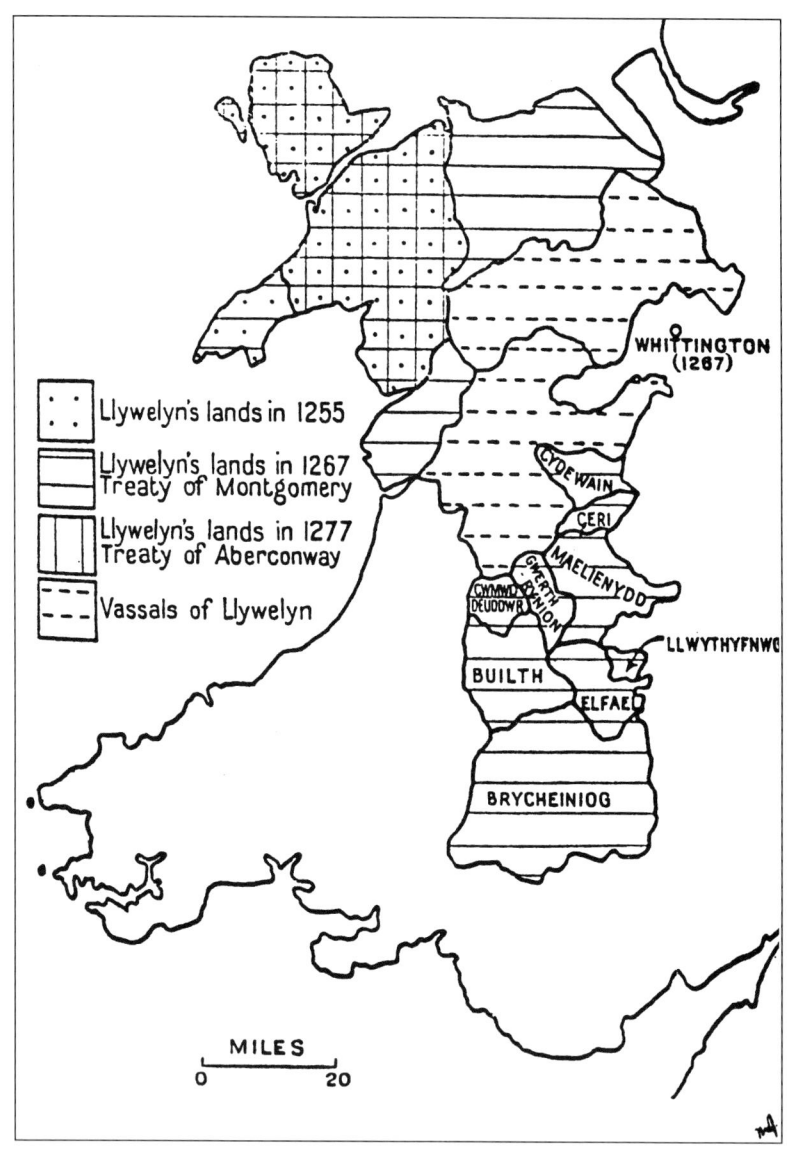

Llywelyn's lands in 1255

Llywelyn's lands in 1267
Treaty of Montgomery

Llywelyn's lands in 1277
Treaty of Aberconway

Vassals of Llywelyn

WHITTINGTON
(1267)

CYDEWAIN

CERI

MAELIENYDD

GWERTHRYNION

CWMWD
DEUDDWR

LLWYTHYFNWG

BUILTH

ELFAEL

BRYCHEINIOG

MILES

0   20

Llywelyn's territories, 1255-77.

his as a result of the death of his vassal, Maredudd. This acquisition was followed by the invasion and conquest of Perfeddwlad, the land between the Conway river and the earldom of Chester. He then marched south to Llanbadarn Fawr, and seized that part of Ceredigion belonging to the King's heir, the Lord Edward, and the area of Builth held by the Mortimers. Roger Mortimer was driven from Gwerthrynion and, early in 1257, Gruffydd ap Gwenwynwyn was expelled from southern Powys. Llywelyn entered Deheubarth, and ravaged mercilessly the lands of the English lords of Kidwelly, Gower, and Swansea. These impressive military successes were made possible by the weakness of the English Crown and the disunity amongst the marcher lords. Llywelyn had now emerged as the undoubted champion of the Welsh against the English, and was master of Wales from the outskirts of Carmarthen to the hinterland of Chester, and from Anglesey to the Brecon Beacons. The other Welsh princes had been compelled to transfer their allegiance from the King to him, and in 1258 he declared himself Prince of Wales, and at an assembly held that year the Welsh lords bound themselves to him in homage and fealty. During the next few years Llywelyn raided the territories of marcher lords, and gained the homage of their Welsh inhabitants. He sided with Simon de Montfort in the struggle of the English barons against the Crown and, despite de Montfort's death at Evesham in 1265, Llywelyn's objectives were to be realised in the Treaty of Montgomery, 1267. This treaty represented the high-water mark of his career; he and his heirs were authorised to hold the title 'Prince of Wales', which meant that he was to receive the homage of all the independent Welsh rulers except Maredudd ap Rhys; he was granted Perfeddwlad, Ceri, Cydewain, Builth, Gwerthrynion, Brecknock, Whittington, and Maelienydd. He was now effectively in control of the greater part of Wales.

His very success was the primary cause of his undoing. The marcher lords now became fully conscious of the danger which Llywelyn represented to themselves, and this appreciation of the threat led to the development of a better understanding between them and the King. Llywelyn's policies had also provoked opposition amongst some of the Welsh lords; and above all, he had incurred the antagonism of his overlord, the King of England.

Until 1272, despite some minor complaints, relations between Llywelyn and the English King were reasonably satisfactory, and Llywelyn continued faithfully to fulfil his obligations under the terms of the treaty of Montgomery. The death of Henry III (1272), however, saw a marked change in Llywelyn's conduct. He left unpaid his annual dues, and refused to obey repeated summonses to swear fealty to the new King, Edward I. According to Llywelyn, redress of grievances had to precede any act of homage. Furthermore, the King was providing refuge for plotters against Llywelyn, and amongst these conspirators was his younger brother, Dafydd. Safe conduct had not been guaranteed, and Eleanor, the daughter of Simon de Montfort, whom Llywelyn wished to marry, had been seized by Edward when she was sailing from France to Wales. To Edward I, on the other hand, these grievances appeared to be frivolous.

Llywelyn's behaviour during this period has been the subject of severe criticism, even condemnation, because he was undoubtedly playing with fire. Possibly his conduct of affairs was dictated by the fact that he was a man of action and not a statesman; he should, perhaps, have devoted these years to consolidating his position. It could be that he had misjudged the political situation, and thought that a revival of baronial opposition to the King was imminent; perhaps he had been carried away by his earlier successes, and was suffering from an inflated ego. What is certain is that he was obsessed by a sense of grievance.

His actions could not be ignored by Edward I, one of the ablest of the medieval Kings of England, and from 1276 he launched attacks against the outlying parts of the Principality. But in the summer of 1277 Edward launched a full-scale offensive from Chester. His army advanced along the coast, while a fleet was dispatched to cut off Llywelyn's food supplies from his granary in Anglesey. In face of such overwhelming odds, Llywelyn was forced to capitulate and to accept the humiliating terms of the treaty of Aberconway. He was stripped of territory; all the lands which he had gained in 1267 were lost, including his gains in mid-Wales—Brecon, Builth, Gwerthrynion, Ceri, Cydewain, and south Powys. The Principality which he had created was destroyed; all that remained to him was Gwynedd west of the river Conway, and for that he had to pay an annual tribute of 1,000 marks.[7] Though he retained the homage of the five lords of Gwynedd, he was no longer overlord of the other independent rulers of Wales. The English king was now to be their overlord as in the days before 1267. Llywelyn could still be addressed as 'Prince of Wales', though it was now an empty title, shorn of any meaning. Finally, the Welsh prince had to pay homage to Edward and, at Christmas 1277, he travelled to London for that purpose. His followers stayed at Islington, where they became objects of derision and fun because of their appearance and uncouth habits.

Though Llywelyn appeared to be genuinely anxious to atone for his acts of defiance, there were still grounds for dispute between himself and the English sovereign. In his vastly extended dominions in Wales, which made Edward I the greatest single landowner in the country, English officials, by their acts of petty tyranny and high-handed behaviour, had incurred the wrath of the Welsh. They performed their duties with excessive zeal and insufficient regard for the feelings of the people under their control. There were, in particular, many disputes about land arising from the war of independence of 1277 and the treaty of Aberconway. The most important, and certainly the most delicate, was the dispute between Llywelyn and his old enemy, Gruffydd ap Gwenwynwyn, the ruler of southern Powys. They both claimed land in Arwystli, which was a kind of buffer zone between them. Llywelyn wanted the dispute settled according to Welsh law; Gruffydd, supported by Edward I, wanted it settled by English law. Before the quarrel could be resolved, the war of 1282 had intervened.

Prince and people, then, were dissatisfied and, in 1282, Llywelyn's brother, Dafydd, no less, he who had supported the English in 1277, and been rewarded for his efforts, raised the standard of rebellion, and assaults were made on the castles of Hawarden, Flint, and Rhuddlan. Revolts then followed throughout Wales; and Oswestry and Llanbadarn, and the castles at Llandovery and Carreg Cennen, were attacked. Llywelyn, as the indisputable national leader, had no option but to throw in his lot with the rebels.

Following initial success in the north, where an English force, crossing from Anglesey to the mainland by means of a pontoon bridge, was cut to pieces, Llywelyn marched south to overrun Powys and the district around Builth. It could be that he wished to reassert his ascendancy in an area which had once been his; on the other hand, it is possible that he was lured south by false promises of support. There was treachery in the air, and the Mortimers, doubtless, were deeply involved. Llywelyn prepared to attack the town and castle of Builth, but between himself and his objectives lay the river Irfon. This river was spanned by a bridge, and Llywelyn dispatched a force to seize and hold it. However, the English did not wait to be attacked. They discovered an undefended ford further up the river, and sent a party across it to fall on the Welsh from the rear, the classic pincer movement. The attack was a complete success, and the bridge was retaken. The main body of the English forces now crossed over and attacked the Welsh army, which was occupying rising ground north of the river. Llywelyn, who had left his headquarters with one companion to proceed to a prearranged rendezvous—it could be that he wished to establish the degree of support he could expect from the local Welsh—hearing the tumult of battle, hurried back to rejoin his men. However, he and his squire were spotted emerging from a small dingle, and both were killed. It was an ignoble end to a colourful career. Both men would have been easy prey, for they were not wearing any body armour. The date was 11 December 1282.

Stephen de Frankton, the English knight generally credited with having run Llywelyn and his companion through with his lance, did not realise that he had killed the Prince of Wales. It was only later that the body was identified. Llywelyn's head was then cut off, washed, and sent to Edward I at Rhuddlan. It was exhibited to the troops, and then dispatched in triumph to London to be placed on public display. Meanwhile, the headless corpse was interred in the Cistercian abbey of Cwm Hir. But though the body may lie 'a mouldering' in its grave there, it is undoubtedly true that his dauntless spirit goes marching on.[8]

Over six hundred years elapsed before the first public monument was erected at Cilmery to the memory of a truly gallant Prince of

Wales. It was in 1902, largely on the initiative of a local squire, S. P. M. Bligh, that an obelisk, twelve feet high, of Llanelwedd stone, was raised at Cefn-y-bedd. Fittingly, it was erected on the fringe of the dingle where, according to tradition, Llywelyn had met his end.

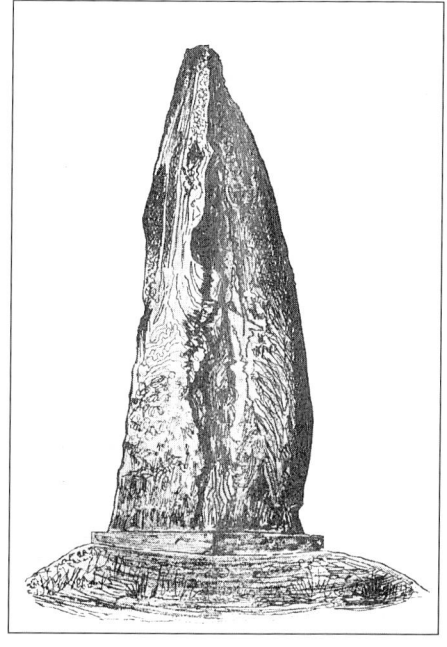

The memorial of 1956.

Bligh died without issue in 1949, and the monument and site at Cefn-y-bedd, by Deed of Gift from the Trustees, came into the possession of Breconshire County Council. The inadequacy of the old monument was generally recognised, and events moved quickly to procure the raising of a more fitting memorial to Llywelyn. The principal driving force behind the new movement was Sir John Lloyd of Dinas, the secretary of the Brecknock Society, and an influential member of Breconshire County Council. He placed certain proposals before the Council in 1952, which received the immediate approval of that body. A national appeal for contributions was launched, and a committee of fourteen, chaired by Major-General Raikes, was established to co-ordinate effort and provide direction.

It soon became clear that the memorial desired was a granite monolith, rough hewn, and standing about fifteen feet high on a circular grassed mound measuring approximately thirty feet in diameter and five feet in height. It was also decided that the monolith should be of grey granite, hewn from the Trefor quarries in Caernarvonshire of the Penmaenmawr Welsh Granite Company Ltd. It was estimated that the total cost would be in the region of £1,750.

Though there was a steady trickle of contributions to the fund, the response to the appeal was far from being enthusiastic. Furthermore, the committee suffered a severe loss in 1954 through the death of Sir John Lloyd. However, it was greatly cheered by the gift of the monolith by the Caernarvonshire County Council.

By 1956 all was ready for the official unveiling. The small original obelisk had been replaced by a massive ten-ton stone; the mound had been turfed; thirteen young oak trees, one for each of the counties of Wales, had been planted, and the oak barrier and gateway had been raised. On Saturday 23 June 1956, in blazing sunshine, the new Prince Llywelyn Memorial was unveiled by Major-General Raikes, Lord Lieutenant of the County of Brecknock, and President of the Brecknock Society, in the presence of vast numbers of the great and the good drawn from all over Wales and representative of all sections of the community. Presiding over proceedings was the Archdruid, Dyfnallt (the Rev. J. Dyfnallt Owen). It was most fitting that he should do so for he, as much as anyone, symbolised the Welsh genius in all its rich and varied manifestations.

Abandoning the giant grey monolith to its silent vigil over the dingle where a noble Welsh Prince met an untimely death, we return to Builth. From there we follow the B4520 which takes us over the Epynt mountain. At Penrhiw, we turn sharp right, and follow the B4519 for three miles until we reach the Drovers' Arms. Here we can see quite clearly the drovers' road leading from Tregaron to Erwood and beyond.

The drovers (*porthmyn*) bought cattle, sheep, pigs, and even geese, at fairs and farms all over Wales. They were usually taken on trust, sold at the English fairs, and the farmers paid on the drovers' return. However, with the emergence of banks like Wilkins' Bank or the 'Old Bank' at Brecon (1778), some drovers borrowed money to enable them to have ready capital to trade. On receipt of their promissory notes, the banks would advance money to them for two or three months. The cattle had to be shod before being driven in noisy cavalcades overland to England, and the preparation of the iron shoes provided blacksmiths with steady work during the winter months. Geese, on the other hand, were walked through wet

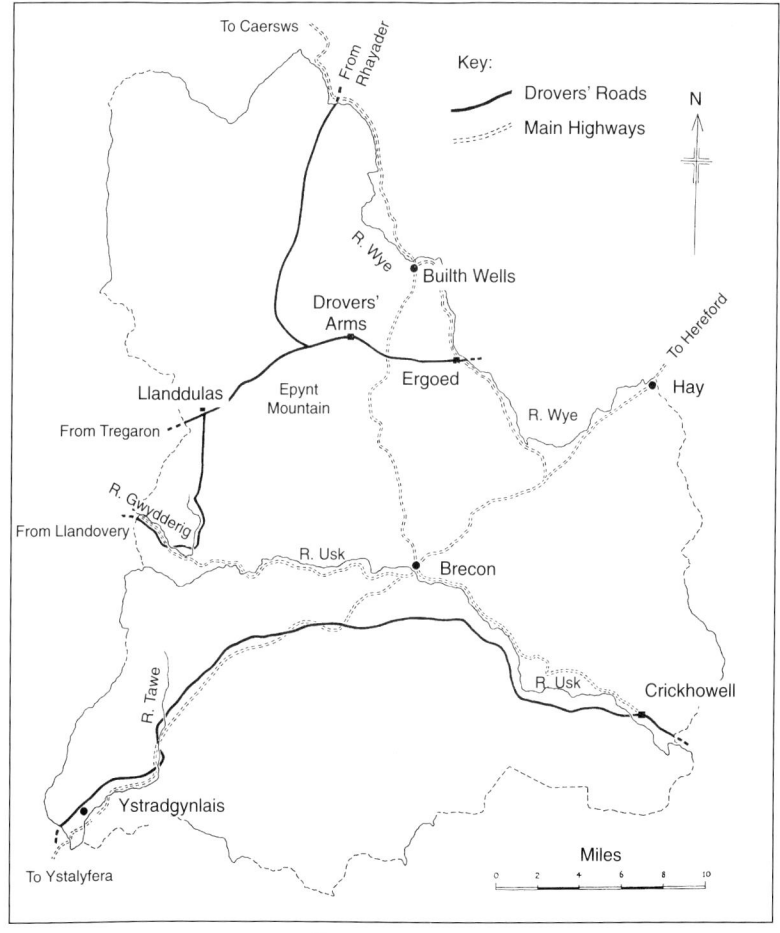

Drovers' roads.

69

tar or pitch. The drove could be heard from many miles away with the whistling and the shouting of the men and the boys, the barking of dogs, the thunder of countless hoofs, and the lowing of the cattle or the bleating of the sheep. Wherever possible, the drovers avoided the turnpike roads, since following those highways would have meant the payment of tolls at the numerous gates scattered along their lengths. But they also avoided the main road in order to follow what they considered to be the most direct route, and to protect the animals' hoofs. Hence they travelled along ridge-top routes and old mountain paths, often referred to as Welsh Ways, covering about twenty miles a day. When it grew dark, the drovers were guided across country by beacons. They rested at inns located along the roads, though some slept out under the stars, where they could fall victim to robbers who would deprive them of their purses. During these respites the cattle and sheep were provided with opportunities to graze. One of these inns was the Drovers' Arms situated on the Epynt mountain which has now been completely renovated.

Drovers' Arms, Epynt Mountain.

Once in England, the cattle—despite the importance of sheep, cattle were, undoubtedly, the backbone of the Welsh rural economy —were fattened on the lush pastures of the Midlands and the southern counties before being taken to the markets at Barnet and Smithfield. Following sale there, they were butchered to feed ever-increasing urban populations, and particularly those of major cities like London and Bristol.

Drovers had existed in Wales from very early times. They were useful even in the manorial economy of the marcher lordships and, in 1349, twenty drovers had taken over four hundred head of cattle from Brecon to replenish Humphrey de Bohun's larder at Pleshy in Essex. The Council in Wales and the Marches, sitting at Ludlow, before its jurisdiction was brought virtually to an end in 1642, was constantly being asked to deal with problems arising from this trafficking in cattle. One problem was cattle stealing, and detection of the rustlers was very difficult; the other was overstocking of the commons in summer with the result that it was not possible to maintain many cattle on them in the winter. The English Civil Wars in the seventeenth century had caused serious dislocation to the trade in cattle to England. Such was the distress that, in 1643, the drovers and clothiers presented a petition to Charles I calling for free passage through his armies with their cattle, sheep, and cottons. The importance of the trade is reflected in Archbishop John Williams's classic comment that the drovers were to Wales what the Spanish galleons had been to Spain, 'bringing thither that little gold and silver we have'. However, the Irish Cattle Act 1666, which prohibited the import of livestock from Ireland, created an insatiable demand for Welsh meat, and by the middle of the eighteenth century it has been estimated that 30,000 cattle and sheep were exported to England annually.

Many of the drovers were wealthy and even cultured men. Some were known to have tried their hands at versifying. They constituted a kind of umbilical cord between the rural areas of Wales and London, since they brought back with them from the capital not only large amounts of ready money, but also the latest fashions, gossip, news, and even melodies. Since movement along the turnpikes could be very hazardous, and the unwary traveller could easily be asked to stand and deliver by a highwayman, many of those who ventured on to the highways even preferred to travel in their company.

To qualify for an annual licence from Quarter Sessions to trade, and married men alone need apply, drovers had to be literate, numerate, and above thirty years of age. Today, there is a tendency to view the drovers through rose-coloured spectacles. However, droving was anything but romantic; it was a filthy and dangerous occupation. Though the majority of the drovers were doubtless men of the greatest integrity—they would hardly have survived for as long as they did had they not been so—there were black sheep amongst them in plenty, and Welsh authors like Ellis Wynne and Twm o'r Nant castigated them as brawling, dishonest fellows. Other critics joined in the chorus and branded them as highwaymen and thieves, and court records reveal cases of blatant betrayal of trust, with some drovers disappearing to Ireland, taking with them money which rightfully belonged to needy Welsh farmers.

Some of the drovers settled as graziers in Leicestershire and Northamptonshire, a move which enabled them to capitalise on the profits that could be made from fattening cattle, which doubled their value. Others, those endowed with some degree of financial acumen, turned to banking, and it was in this fashion that *Banc yr Eidion Du* (The Bank of the Black Ox) at Llandovery, and *Banc y Ddafad Ddu* (The Bank of the Black Sheep) came into existence.

However, in the nineteenth century, another strand in the rich weave of the Welsh social fabric was destroyed, when the chug of the steam engine made itself heard in the Principality. The onset of steam had certainly led to the decay of the canals; but it also led to the disappearance of the drovers. They could not compete, since the movement of animals by rail was far quicker, easier, and cheaper than by road. It is undoubtedly true that there must be movement in society otherwise it will die. Unfortunately, with technological advance there is always a price to pay, and in the case of the harnessing of steam, a human victim was the drover.

We will now leave the Drovers' Arms and the drovers' road to their memories of a more 'romantic' yesteryear, and return to Brecon. There, at leisure, we can relive in our imaginations the experiences of the day: the hum of the turbines at Elston's garage in the Struet, the roar of the furnace on the banks of the Honddu, the stark majesty of the tower at Bronllys, the poignancy associated with the monolith at Cefn-y-bedd, and the flickering shadows of noisy men and beasts slowly plodding their way eastwards along highland roads. Tomorrow is another day, but on this occasion we will not travel far, for the town and its immediate environs will be the focus of our attention.

NOTES

[1] The factory has now been removed and replaced by a garden dedicated to the memory of E. W. Williamson, third bishop of Swansea and Brecon.

[2] He subsequently moved to the 'Greyhound' in the Struet, and from there to the 'Blue Boar' in the Watton.

[3] The palace on the brow of the hill.

[4] Supra, p. 41.

[5] He was a great admirer of Dafydd ap Gwilym and avidly collected his poetic output.

[6] The engraving is incorrect. Evidently it was composed of two sketches drawn from different points of view.

[7] £666 13s. 4d.

[8] There is still uncertainty concerning the facts of Llywelyn's death. I have adopted the generally accepted version, but not all historians would accept this interpretation. See Llinos Smith's reconsideration of this evidence in *Welsh History Review*, 11 (1982-3).

Day 4: Penoyre, Boys' Intermediate School, Priory Church and House; Sir John Price

Today, we shall not venture far, and since the furthest point will be Penoyre, let us start there while we are still completely refreshed after a good night's rest. Penoyre is an impressive mansion situated two miles from Brecon. To get there we take the road to Cradoc. At the crossroads we turn right, and follow the road for about two hundred yards before turning left up a driveway, past the Cradoc Golf and Country Club, to Penoyre House. This is approached through impressive iron gates made by Daniel Rowland, a blacksmith from Tairderwen, and along a delightful avenue of Irish yews.

Penoyre is the anglicised version of the Welsh *Pen Aur* or 'Head of Gold'. The Watkinses of Penoyre were descended from the Watkinses of Pen-y-rhos, Llanigon, Brecknockshire, and the Penoyres of The Moor, Herefordshire. The house at Penoyre, near Cradoc, was begun by the Rev. Thomas Watkins, vicar of Llandefalle and rector of Llandefaelog. He was the son of the founder of the family, Penoyre Watkins (1721-91), who had married Mary, the daughter of David Lloyd of Rhosferig, near Builth. Following her death at the early age of thirty-four in December 1762, the Rhosferig estate came into his possession. Penoyre Watkins moved to Brecon to practise law, and so successful was he that he was able to purchase substantial estates, one being the Broadway estate near Laugharne in Carmarthenshire, from Mary Gwynne of Garth, Breconshire. When Penoyre Watkins died, he left his Carmarthenshire estates to his eldest son, George Pryce Watkins, who had donated £1,000 in 1832 towards the founding of the Brecknock Infirmary. But the principal part of his Breconshire estate was left to his younger son, Thomas.

Thomas Watkins was an accomplished classical scholar and a considerable traveller. He published two volumes on his journeyings in Switzerland, Italy, Sicily, Turkey, Greece, Ragusa, and the Dalmatian Isles, and so successful were these publications that they went into a second edition. In January 1795, at Marylebone Church,

London, he married Susanna Eleanora, the only daughter of Richard Vaughan of Golden Grove, Carmarthenshire. They begat a numerous brood, since there were altogether six children. The eldest son, Penaur, having been lost at sea, the estate at Penoyre descended to the sole remaining son, John Lloyd Vaughan Watkins. He was to play a leading part in the public life of Breconshire, and both the county and the town of Brecon were to benefit from his munificence.

Colonel John Lloyd Vaughan Watkins.

John Lloyd Vaughan Watkins was born in 1802. As was to be expected of a man with his social background, he received a very privileged education, and he studied at Harrow and Christ Church, Oxford. He was twice married, first to Sophia Louisa Henrietta, when he was thirty-one years of age, and secondly, to Eliza Luther, when he was fifty. There were no children from either marriage.

He was generally referred to as Colonel Watkins, as he was commandant of the Breconshire Militia from 1847 to 1865. But civil matters also interested him, and he served as Liberal M.P. for

Brecon on three separate occasions: 1832-4, 1847-52, and from 1854 until his death in 1865. He was a noted reformer, and when a mob, as part of a nationwide agitation for parliamentary reform, roamed the streets of Brecon in 1831 breaking gentlemen's windows, they were heard to shout for 'Watkins and reform'. In 1832, following the enactment of the first Parliamentary Reform Act, he wrested control of the borough seat from C. M. R. Morgan of Tredegar Park, a Conservative, by the narrow margin of 110 votes to 104. He had earlier shown an interest in the county seat, and at the general election of 1831, he had opposed Thomas Wood of Gwernyfed, though he had withdrawn after the first day's poll, when Wood already had a lead of 282 votes to 138. Wood continued to represent the county until his retirement in 1847.[1] In the borough, the Morgan family regained the borough seat in the elections of 1835, 1837, and 1841, only for Colonel Watkins to win it back in 1847. However, he lost it again to a Morgan in 1852, but regained the seat in 1854, and then retained it until 1865.

Apart from representing Brecon in Parliament, he was public-spirited in other respects as well. Thus, he was a local councillor, and when the reformed corporation came into existence following the passing of the Municipal Corporations Act 1835, Colonel Watkins was the first mayor of Brecon elected under the terms of the act. That was in 1836. When the new corporation established a Board of Health, one of the members of the Board was again Colonel Watkins. A freemason, he became Worshipful Master of the old Loyal Cambrian Lodge at Brecon. Other offices held by him included those of Justice of the Peace, High Sheriff of the County (1836), and Lord Lieutenant (1847-65). In addition, he held the patronage of three church livings, and for some years supported a day school at Battle village, paying the schoolmaster £20 a year, a sum which was augmented by fees amounting to approximately £8.

When Colonel Watkins inherited his father's estate, he decided to enlarge and beautify the family home with a view to making it a residence fit to entertain royalty. Royalty never came, but the extensions were on such a scale that he practically rebuilt the old house. It was a restructuring that involved him in enormous expense, and it is estimated that he expended £100,000 on his new mansion. In his diaries he notes meticulously the progress made, and the cost of every individual item down to the last brick. Several ornamental lakes were provided in the landscaped grounds, and these were well-stocked with fish. His guests, who came from all over the county, were thus provided with many a pleasurable hour by the lakesides. A farm adjacent to the mansion still bears the name Pysgodlyn (Fish Lake).

Penoyre in the days of Col. J. L. V. Watkins.

However, the Colonel's ambitious plans for his mansion together with its upkeep thereafter, his generosity—he was a most liberal contributor towards the Brecon Infirmary—and the burden of heavy taxes, placed an altogether too severe strain on his financial resources. Necessity finally compelled him to abandon his mansion, and move into the 'Bear Hotel'² in Ship Street, Brecon. His last days were spent in comparative poverty, but until the end he retained the respect and affection of the people of Brecon, who remembered his years of unselfish public service, and his great

78

generosity to his friends and the locality. His funeral in 1865 was attended with much military and civil ceremonial, and attracted an extremely large gathering, a demonstration of public regard for a great benefactor of the local community. He was interred in the family vault at Llandefaelog, and a tablet to his memory can be seen in Battle Church. The major part of his entailed estates passed to his cousin George, son of Major Walter Rice of Llwyn-y-Brain, Carmarthenshire, who assumed the name Watkins in addition to Rice. By the terms of the will of his father, Thomas Watkins, the remaining parts were inherited by his three sisters, who then bequeathed their portions of his estate to their eldest sons.

Nothing is known of the fate of Penoyre mansion between the time of its abandonment by Colonel Watkins until its sale by public auction in 1868. Was it left untenanted, was it leased, or was there a kind of resident caretaker? On Thursday, 29 October 1868, the Penoyre estate, which was quite substantial, was offered for sale at the Castle Hotel, Brecon, by W. A. Bowler of London. Twenty-four lots were placed on auction. Some were not sold, as they failed to reach the reserve price; others were sold to local buyers. However, Lot 1, described in the report in the *Brecon County Times* as 'The Pennoyre Mansion, with park and Bettin plantations, etc' was knocked down to Matthew John Rhodes, Esq., of Allan, for £24,000. The entire proceeds from the property sold amounted to £44,880.

It is doubtful whether Rhodes ever took up residence in the house. Certainly, when the Rev. Francis Kilvert, curate of Clyro, Radnorshire, visited the mansion in August 1870, he commented in his now celebrated diary on the silence which pervaded the deserted house and grounds, the weed-covered paths, and the general state of neglect with everything overgrown. Possibly, Rhodes was a speculator who only bought the property to fell the trees—the property was rich in standing timber—and thus make a quick and substantial profit. On the other hand, it is likely that the sale was never completed, and that the house remained vacant until it was purchased by Baron Cleasby.

According to John de Winton, a solicitor, and a member of the long-established de Winton family, it was his grandfather, William de Winton, of Maesderwen, Llanfrynach, who first brought Penoyre to the attention of Baron Cleasby. It happened in 1874, during William de Winton's year in office as High Sheriff of Breconshire. Cleasby, as one of the Barons of the Court of Exchequer, had come to Brecon to hold the Assizes. The High Sheriff had taken the opportunity to show him Penoyre, and Cleasby was so impressed by what he saw that he decided to buy the mansion and its associated properties, which included lands, farms, houses and cottages. The purchase price was believed to have been £45,500.

On the death of Sir Anthony Cleasby on 6 October 1879, the estate was inherited by his son, Richard Digby Cleasby. Educated at Eton and Cambridge, he was called to the Bar at the Inner Temple in 1864. He played a prominent role in the life of the county, as he was a member of Breconshire County Council, Chairman of the Quarter Sessions, and a liberal contributor to the funds of the Brecon Infirmary and the Breconshire Agricultural Society. High Sheriff of Breconshire in 1890, he also patronised the Brecon Literary Institution. This institution, which was, in addition, a lending library, was located at No. 33, The Watton. The librarian was T. Hadley Watkins, and the secretary was his brother, Oscar. Christ College, too, benefited from Cleasby's liberality, since the greater part of the cost of re-flooring the chapel in oak was met from his purse; he also made a substantial contribution towards the cost of the oak choir stalls. It was during R. D. Cleasby's occupation of Penoyre that the house was re-roofed. He considered the slate slabs to be too heavy—some of them weighed about one hundredweight—and, therefore, too dangerous, so he decided to have them replaced entirely by smaller and lighter slates. A further innovation was the re-location of the lodge, and the construction of a new driveway. The original lodge had occupied a position adjacent to a wood, and the house had been approached through these trees, an eerie experience at night. Those who approached the house on foot could also get wet, as a considerable amount of water would accumulate on the driveway. On the death of R. D. Cleasby in 1909, his wife moved to the south of England, and Lucy Antonia McClintock, daughter of Baron Cleasby, and sister of Richard, took up residence.

The McClintocks were excellent employers, and the large staff at the house was treated with the utmost consideration and kindness. Husband and wife were great lovers of music, and the husband was also an enthusiastic carpenter. The winter months were spent in London, and some of the servants, to the great regret of the local Romeos, would accompany them, leaving Penoyre in the care of a skeleton staff. While living at 2, Ormond Gate, London, produce and flowers for their use would be sent regularly from the estate to the City by train. But the peaceful routine at Penoyre was now to be rudely disturbed with the outbreak of the First World War, when the house became a convalescent hospital for soldiers wounded on the Western Front. The McClintocks still retained a few rooms for their own personal use when they were not in London, and Mrs McClintock was accustomed to visit the wounded to build up morale.

Among the patients at Penoyre were a few local men. One was Tom Close, who later became mine host at the 'Boar's Head' situated at the bottom of Ship Street; another was Jim Watkins of Rhydybernard Terrace; Ernest Howells, a skilled plasterer, was also there, and he recalled being met at Brecon railway station by Nancy Jones of Tredurn, Glamorgan Street, an ambulance driver. He was a patient in Patti ward, so called because it had been endowed by the famous soprano, Adelina Patti, of Craig-y-nos. She also provided the hospital with a billiard table, a most acceptable and popular gift which was in constant use. But the patients were not solely concerned with pleasurable pastimes; they were also involved in useful activities such as handicraft, making black cats from felt removed from gentlemen's bowler hats, raffia summer hats, and necklaces. On pleasant sunny days they would experience a change of environment, as outdoor excursions were arranged in one of Harold Elston's vehicles, or in the hospital basket trap drawn by a donkey.[3]

Most of the nursing staff at Penoyre comprised different detachments of the Breconshire Red Cross: Crickhowell detachment would serve for one month, Glasbury another, then Brecon, and so on. To their credit, and as far as can be ascertained, only one patient was lost, and this unfortunate was buried in Battle churchyard.

Penoyre outing for wounded soldiers. (courtesy of A. Elston)

Presiding over the nursing staff was the matron, Hyett Williams, of the Struet, Brecon; and the chief medical officer was a greatly respected Brecon doctor, Valentine Rees. 'County' ladies were very much in evidence in the administration of the hospital, and prominent in their ranks were Lady Glanusk, Lady Lloyd, Mrs Maybery,[4] Mrs McClennan, the Hon. Dulcie Bailey, and the Misses Blanche and Judith Butler of Glasbury.

Much of the food for the wounded 'Tommies' was provided from the farms and gardens of the estate. A Miss Mary Lloyd, the dairy maid, made fresh butter, bread and cakes, while George Weeks, the head gardener, ensured a constant and regular supply of fresh vegetables and fruit. However, in 1918, on the cessation of hostilities, the house reverted to being a private residence again, and the old routine was restored. Mrs McClintock continued to reside at Penoyre even after her husband's death—he was buried in Ireland—but the social whirl began to fade, even though she still entertained her closest friends and promoted charitable causes. When she died in London on 30 April 1939, at a ripe old age, the community at Brecon and Cradoc had lost a good friend.

Penoyre now came into the possession of another relative, John Hill, a teacher living in Norfolk. Just before the outbreak of war in

1939 he, his wife, and three children travelled to Penoyre intending to stay for one month. The outbreak of the Second World War resulted in an intended stay of one month being extended to seven years. The threat of invasion led John Hill to invite Taversham Preparatory School, at which he had once taught, to remove to Penoyre and occupy the empty spaces there. The invitation was accepted, and the school remained at Penoyre until suitable premises were found nearer Norfolk. The next threat from Hitler's Germany were the 'doodle-bugs', the V1s and V2s, and the house now accommodated large numbers of refugees fleeing from the new threat from the sky.

When peace returned in 1945, the Hills were not able to keep Penoyre. Death duties and huge maintenance costs made that impossible. And so, in 1946/7, the mansion and parkland immediately surrounding it were sold to Merthyr Corporation, who used the house as a school for delicate children. It was administered by the County Borough of Merthyr Tydfil Education Committee in co-operation with the Education Committees of the counties of Brecon and Radnor, and a small number of pupils from these two counties were allowed to attend the school.

In 1967 Merthyr Corporation sold the mansion and 123 acres of parkland to the Cradoc Golf and Country Club. Since then the mansion has changed hands several times, and currently, the house is a nursing home for the elderly.

Its past glories faded, let us now leave Penoyre House and return to Brecon, again via Cradoc Road. Near the bottom of the hill, on the left-hand side, and overlooking the road, is a red-brick building. This was once home to the Brecon Boys' Grammar School. The school was a product of the Welsh Intermediate Act of 1889, which represented the government's response to the Aberdare Report, 1881, on the state of intermediate and higher education in Wales. By the act the new County Councils, which had made their début in 1888, were empowered to raise a ½d. rate to fund secondary education, and the Treasury was to make a grant to each county equivalent to the amount raised. The building of new Intermediate Schools had become essential as a result of the booming population

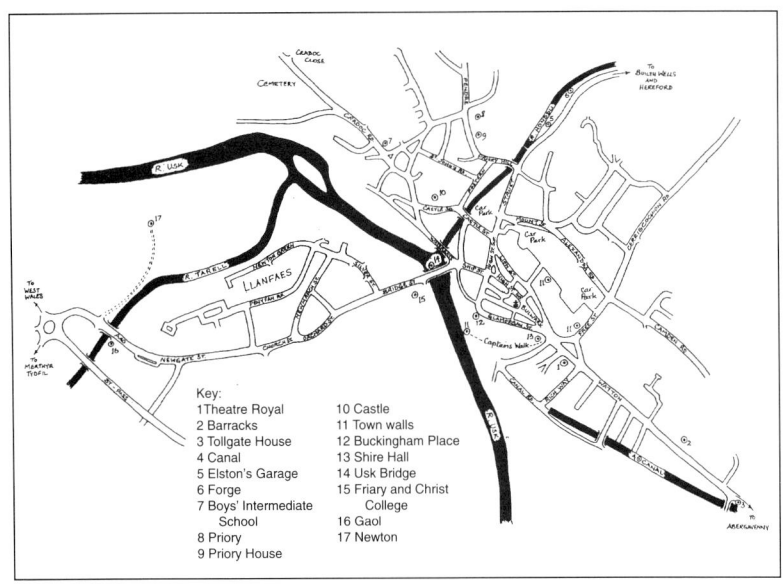

Location of places of historical interest within Brecon.

Key:
1 Theatre Royal
2 Barracks
3 Tollgate House
4 Canal
5 Elston's Garage
6 Forge
7 Boys' Intermediate
   School
8 Priory
9 Priory House
10 Castle
11 Town walls
12 Buckingham Place
13 Shire Hall
14 Usk Bridge
15 Friary and Christ
   College
16 Gaol
17 Newton

The Boys' Intermediate School at Cradoc Road.

84

of Victorian Wales, and also because the country was now being provided with her own university colleges. The first of these colleges, Aberystwyth, had opened its doors in 1872, to be followed shortly afterwards by Cardiff (1883), and Bangor in the following year; and before these colleges could function properly, more secondary schools were required to prepare students for admission.

At Brecon it was not until 1895 that it was resolved, at a meeting of the school managers of the Brecon County School District, held in Mount Street Primary School, with the mayor of the borough, J. A. Jebb, in the chair, to build two separate secondary schools, one for the boys and another for the girls. This decision to build state secondary schools was strongly opposed by certain elements within the town, especially the Nonconformists, who felt that the proper response should be for Christ College to admit local children. A site for the building of the proposed schools was now acquired from the Marquis of Camden in Cradoc Road, but before building commenced it dawned upon the powers that be that the site was too distant from the station for 'any but the strongest girls'. In the light of this revelation, the decision was taken to build the girls' school on a site on Cerrig Cochion Hill much nearer the station.

While the School Managers were giving consideration to the building of the new schools, temporary accommodation was found for the boys in two rooms at Dr Coke's Methodist Church in Lion Street (the site is now occupied by Leo's store). Mr Nathan John B.A. (London), second master at the Pembroke Dock Intermediate School, was appointed Headmaster at an annual salary of £150, together with a capitation allowance. His assistant was Thomas Butcher, formerly headmaster of what he called 'The Middle Class School'. This was a private school catering mainly for the sons of Nonconformists, and it has to be appreciated that in the latter half of the nineteenth century the church had been overwhelmed by an irresistible Nonconformist tide. When the school was opened on Tuesday, 22 September, 1896 there were 47 pupils on roll, a few of whom were boarders. For the neighbours this sudden appearance of so many boys at their doorsteps was not without its problems, and soon complaints were received by the Managers concerning the 'nuisance of noise' as the boys entered and left the school.

Unlike the situation today, pupils then had to pay fees and these included: tuition, £5; boarding, not to exceed £30; Music, £2 5s.; stationery and the use of textbooks, 7s.6d. each. Science and Technical subjects were well represented on the curriculum, and the physical welfare of the pupils was certainly not ignored as part of the Recreation Field was leased at £5 a year for school games. In November 1899, a final determination was made in respect of the tenders submitted for the building of the boys' and girls' schools. It was decided to accept that of £5,681 plus fees for both schools submitted by E. Groom of Port Talbot, and the completed boys' school was officially opened at Cradoc Road on 10 July 1901 by Charles Morley M.P.

By 1958, because the accommodation at the school at Cradoc Road had become completely inadequate, and owing much to the energy of a new Director of Education, Deiniol Williams, a more modern Brecon Boys' Grammar-Technical School was opened on a magnificent site at Penlan. But it was not to remain a grammar school for much longer, as in 1971, because of the nationwide disillusionment with the 11+ entrance examination, Breconshire, rather belatedly as compared with other authorities, reorganised education at Brecon on comprehensive lines. The three secondary schools occupying sites on Penlan Hill, the Brecon Boys' Grammar School, the Brecon Girls' Grammar School, and Brecon Secondary Modern-Technical School were merged into one school, Brecon High School, and Mr Aneurin Rees, M.Sc., a product of Swansea University College, and headmaster of the Brecon Boys' Grammar School, was appointed to take the helm.

The old Boys' Grammar School at Cradoc has rather a forlorn aspect about it in the daytime, as though it still mourned the absence of its former occupants. However, in the evenings, it comes alive and echoes, once again, to the sound of young voices, because the building is now a Youth Centre. Enough is enough: it is time for us to leave and proceed to the Priory Church of St John the Evangelist, which we reach by turning left at the Cwm Inn.

The Priory Church is a very ancient foundation. It was established by the Norman conqueror of Brecknock, Bernard de Newmarch, shortly after his victory in 1093 over the local ruler, Bleddyn ap Maenarch, loyally supported by his overlord and brother-in-law, Rhys ap Tewdwr, the King of Deheubarth (south-west Wales). On that fateful day, both Bleddyn and Rhys were slain, and the scene of the conflict was possibly Battle, some three miles to the north-west of Brecon.

It was on the advice of his confessor, Roger, a monk of Battle Abbey, Sussex, who was then officiating as chaplain at the castle, and also as an expression of his gratitude to the Almighty for having blessed his military enterprises with success, that Bernard built a priory at Brecon. The site of the original church, possibly built of wood, might well have been within the castle bailey for, according to the foundation charter, it was 'situated in (or at) my castle of Honddu'. Within the castle bailey, five burgages were granted to it; in itself a clear indication that a town in embryo had already made its appearance. Town and church could not have been in closer proximity, and it was only later that the church retreated to its present location outside the castle, though within bowshot of its walls. The nascent town, if it was to grow and prosper, could not possibly remain within the castle bailey, and it also now migrated to the eastern bank of the Honddu.

When the church was rebuilt, 'from the foundations', on its present location, Roger, assisted by a fellow monk, Walter, added domestic buildings, and on their completion they were joined by other monks. Bernard constituted the church a cell of the newly-founded Benedictine abbey of Battle, which thus became the mother church of the new foundation. The priory was liberally endowed by Bernard and his followers. Bernard's gifts included, in England, lands in Herefordshire, Staffordshire and Somerset and, locally, the churches of Talgarth and Llangorse, a portion of the tithes of Llansantffraed, together with those of Hay; a carucate of land adjoining a mill on the river Usk, and two-thirds of another upon the Honddu; the chapel of St Nicholas within the castle, lands at Llangasty and Llynfi, and five burgages in Brecon. Until the middle of the thirteenth century successive lords of Brecon, such as the de Breoses and the de Bohuns, and their feudal tenants, were liberal with their gifts. Particularly generous was Roger, earl of

Hereford, who, over a period of eleven years, conferred no fewer than ten charters on the monks. His rule has been described as constituting a 'golden age' in the history of the priory. Even kings and bishops were enrolled among its benefactors. Brecon priory was the second richest Benedictine house in Wales, though it is significant that its grants were not forthcoming from Welsh princes and chieftains. To them the priory was as much an instrument of conquest as the castle and the borough. Until its dissolution in 1538 the Benedictine house at Brecon never succeeded in overcoming local prejudices, and the Black Monks were always recruited from a non-Welsh population. At the end of the thirteenth century the priory had an income of £56 4*s*. 4*d*. from its various properties. By the time of its dissolution in the sixteenth century its valuation was £112. But despite the gifts which it had received, the priory, when compared with other religious orders in Wales, was not well endowed, and when compared with English or Continental houses, it was abysmally poor.

Cathedral Church of St John the Evangelist.

Within the monastic foundation at Brecon the influence of the prior was paramount, and these priors were appointed by, and could be recalled at will by, the abbot of the mother house at Battle. They do not appear to have been men of distinction, and a few even fell from grace, and for that reason attained a certain degree of notoriety. The community over which they presided was not large, since the average number of monks was only four or five, less than half of what it should have been, as the minimum complement required to run a house efficiently was thirteen. However, it has to be admitted that it was very rare for a daughter cell of this kind to have thirteen monks. In addition to the monks, there was a large number of lay servants, and in 1535 these had numbered fifteen. Included in their ranks would have been a janitor and a steward.

In the fourteenth century the priory at Brecon had become gravely impoverished. Indeed, in 1368 it was reported to be in a ruinous condition with its few monks in danger of dispersal. This crisis in the affairs of the priory had arisen from the operation of factors such as the interminable Hundred Years War with France, which had led to increased royal exploitation of the church, and the dire effects of the Black Death of 1349, and the subsequent plagues, which led to a drop in land values and labour shortages. The priory now found it necessary to lease out the nine churches appropriated to it together with the glebe lands. Its five mills also suffered a similar fate. By the late fifteenth and early sixteenth century the priory had adopted a *rentier* economy, i.e. of renting out its lands and resources. There were other pressures on the monastic economy, and amongst these were royal exactions and corrodies.[5]

However, the fifteenth century witnessed some recovery in the fortunes of the Welsh church, and this improvement was reflected, in the latter half of the century, in the building of magnificent towers, screens, and lofts. The 'Golden' rood in Brecon priory was one of its glories; it was of gigantic proportions, and since miraculous healing powers were soon attributed to it—this was an age of superstition—the priory became a noted centre of pilgrimage. Indeed, from at least 1408, the priory was referred to as the 'Church of the Holy Rood', and the house would certainly have profited from the offerings of the pilgrims.

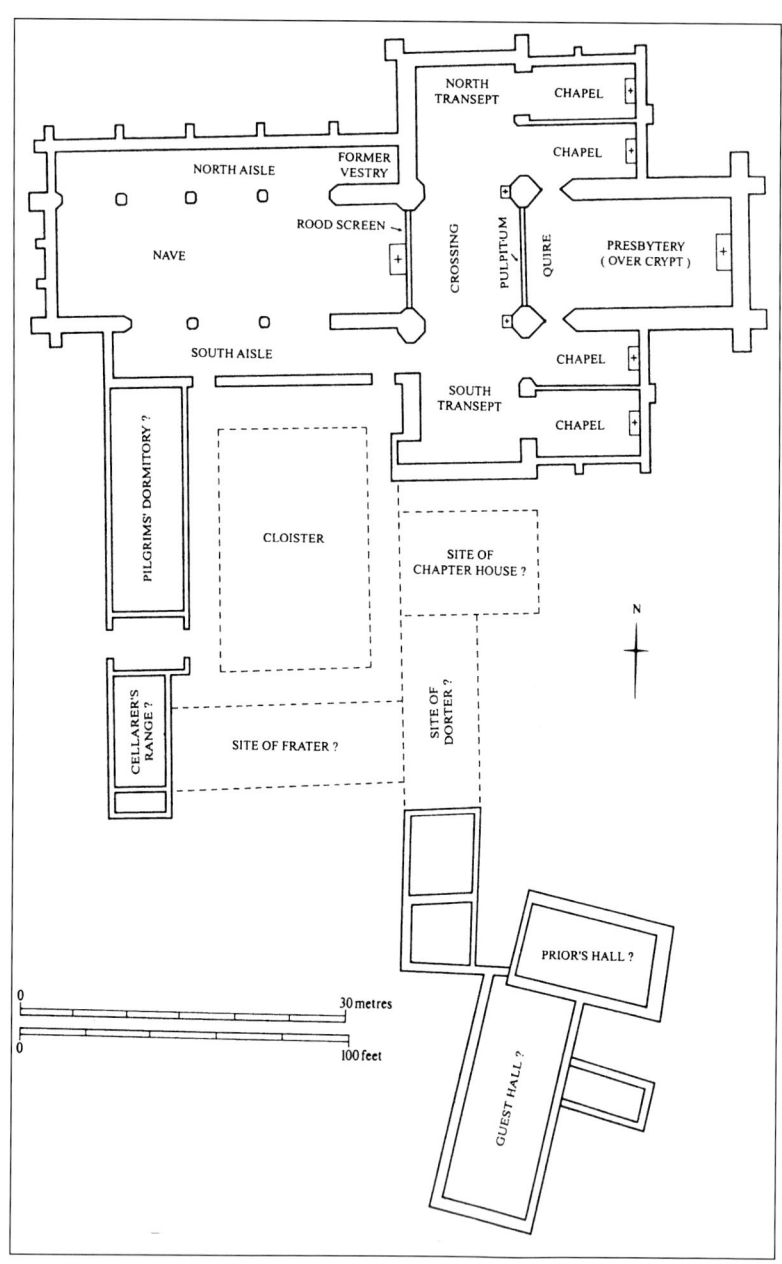

NORTH
TRANSEPT

CHAPEL

CHAPEL

FORMER
VESTRY

NORTH AISLE

ROOD SCREEN

CROSSING

PULPITUM

QUIRE

PRESBYTERY
(OVER CRYPT)

NAVE

SOUTH AISLE

CHAPEL

SOUTH
TRANSEPT

CHAPEL

PILGRIMS' DORMITORY ?

CLOISTER

SITE OF
CHAPTER HOUSE ?

N

CELLARER'S
RANGE ?

SITE OF FRATER ?

SITE OF
DORTER ?

0

30 metres

0

100 feet

PRIOR'S HALL ?

GUEST HALL ?

A conjectural plan of the Priory in the fourteenth century.

90

On the eve of its dissolution in 1538, the priory at Brecon still presented a spectacle of decay. Its lands, mills and appropriated churches had been farmed out to laymen, and the monks were no longer directly involved in the cultivation of the glebe; it was poor; the complement of monks was only six, indicative of the fact that the monastic ideal had lost its attraction. The priors were men of little worth, and were all English. When the end came, it would appear that no voices in Brecon were raised in lamentation. The prior, Robert Halden, and the monks were pensioned off, Halden receiving £16 per annum for life, while the monks were assigned sums varying between £3 10*s*. and £4. The lands of the priory were transferred to the Crown, and then leased out to a local gentleman of considerable repute, Sir John Price.[6] Even the bells and the lead from the roof came under the hammer, and the rood was destroyed. The sale of the bells was to occasion a dispute between the burgesses and the King's commissioners, for the townspeople claimed that three of the five bells belonged to them, and should not be offered for sale. The commissioners, reluctantly, had to agree. In 1538 about seven tons of lead was melted into ingots and sold to be used for various purposes. Sir Roger Vaughan bought six of them to enable repairs to be undertaken to Brecon castle. Another had been used to repair the 'Receiver's chamber in the priory'. The priory silver was also seized, and plate amounting to 496 oz. went to replenish Henry VIII's coffers.

Notwithstanding the pillaging, the building was not reduced to a ruin despite the damage to the roof. Its survival arose from the fact that during the Middle Ages the nave had been used as the parish church, whose vicar had been appointed by the prior. The remainder of the building had been used by the monks. The two parts had been separated by a massive screen some three or four storeys high.

In subsequent centuries the edifice served solely as the parish church, but it was to suffer severely from neglect. Some of the buildings were adapted for domestic purposes, while others were converted to stables. In the eighteenth century the cloisters disappeared. This was some time after the publication of the prospect of Brecon priory by the brothers Buck in 1741. By the beginning of the nineteenth century such was the state of dilapidation that only the nave was in regular use. The church was cold and damp, and the preacher's voice, because of a loud echo, was inaudible in all parts of the church with the exception of a few pews in the immediate vicinity of the pulpit. In 1836 the curate, William North, claimed that the discomfort and danger to health were such that the faint-hearted were leaving the church, attracted by the comfortable, and elegantly fitted, dissenting chapels. Legislation relating to the church in the 1830s and 1840s enabled church resources to be released, and the work of regeneration could commence, particularly the restoration and extension of ancient fabrics. At the priory in Brecon, based on proposals submitted by T. H. Wyatt, rebuilding was begun in 1836, when Lord Camden who, as lay impropriator, was responsible for the chancel, had it reslated. Furthermore, a glass screen was erected between the choir and the nave and, to improve comfort and seating capacity, the church was repewed, with 420 seats appropriated and 271 free. Following 'tinkering' operations between 1836-40 which obliterated some of the most beautiful features of the church, in 1858 Sir Gilbert Scott, one of the foremost restoring architects of the day, submitted his recommendations on what needed to be done. Following in the wake of this report, from 1861, proper restoration work, in the neo-Gothic style, was undertaken, though it was limited to the eastern end of the church—the chancel, tower, transepts and north chapel —and the work was completed in 1862 at a cost of £2,693. The expense was largely met from public subscriptions.

In 1872 Scott produced another report, and between 1873-5 the nave and the aisles were thoroughly renovated at a cost of £5,500. Early in the present century, the tower was in danger of collapse, so W. D. Caröe, who was diocesan architect for St David's, was instructed to prepare plans to strengthen it. Later, the south-east chapels were restored to something resembling their medieval dimensions, and part of the former stables and the domestic wing in the south-west were converted into vestries.

In 1914 the Welsh church was disestablished and partially disendowed, though the outbreak of war meant that implementation of these decisions had to be delayed. It was only in 1920 that the Church in Wales came into being. A diocese of Swansea and

Brecon was formed in 1923, the culmination of discussions which had been going on for years. In the light of this development, Brecon acquired a greatly enhanced importance, since it now became the cathedral church of the new diocese. In consequence, buildings within the precinct of the former priory, which had been transferred to lay hands at the Reformation, were restored either through gift or purchase.[7]

Little remains of the late eleventh-century church which was built on this site. The only evidence for its existence appears to be the font located in the west end of the nave, and a small section of walling. The church, as it is today, is basically thirteenth-century. It was rebuilt then in the Gothic style, beginning at the east end, and the masons employed were mostly English and drawn from the border counties. though there would appear to have been some Welshmen amongst them, people with names like Evan Hen and Grono ap Iohan. There is evidence, such as masons' marks, to suggest that these were the craftsmen who were also employed at Hereford Cathedral. They were all paid the same rate, 6*d.* or 8*d.* a day. The builders at Brecon took as their model the mother church at Battle. This was understandable since the priory, after all, was a cell of that house. Furthermore, for the most part, it was staffed by monks from that abbey, and it is most significant that the hand employed at the famous scriptorium in Brecon priory was based on that used at Battle.

The remodelled church was cruciform in shape and consisted of a nave, chancel, two aisles, and north and south transepts, the whole being straddled by a massive, square, battlemented tower with spire, ninety feet high, which housed the bells. These were last rung in 1802 when Lord Nelson, accompanied by Lady Hamilton, visited the town on his way to Merthyr. After an interval of almost two hundred years, on 8 May 1995, to commemorate VE Day, the bells rang joyfully over the town once again, but it was a vastly augmented peal, as the number of bells had been increased to ten. To accommodate the considerable increase in weight, the tower had to be further strengthened, and the whole exercise proved very costly, amounting to £250,000. Most of the architecture of the present edifice is Early English, though in the late thirteenth and early fourteenth centuries some work was done in the Decorated style, when the nave was extended in length. It was in the aisles of this church that, after the Reformation, the most prominent and prosperous of the trade guilds came to have their chapels. These were five in number: the shoemakers, tailors, weavers, glovers and tuckers.

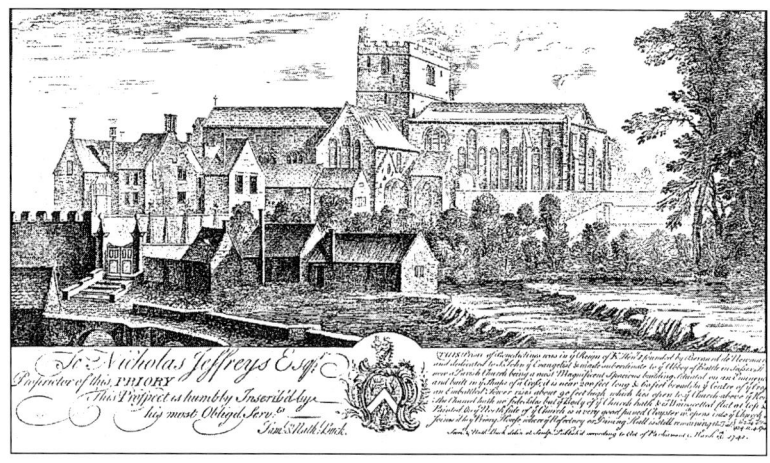

Priory House and Church from the south-east.

Immediately to the south of the present cathedral is the deanery, and it was here that the priors resided, though the building that one looks at today bears little resemblance to the thirteenth century house which they occupied. Central to the medieval house was the hall which was open to the roof. This hall would have had at one end a 'cross-passage' with opposing entrances, and at the other a raised dais, on which was set the high table where the head of the house would entertain his guests. The fire would have been in the centre of the floor, and the smoke would have escaped through the roof. Subsidiary accommodation was provided at the two ends with first floors over them. The service rooms were usually located beyond the cross-passage, and there, food could be stored and prepared; behind the dais, on the other hand, was the solar or private apartments of the family. However, in a large establishment such as a monastery, these arrangements could be duplicated, and this would appear to have been the situation at Brecon, where there is evidence of a second hall having been built at right angles to the first. This addition could well have been the prior's own hall, the other being used to entertain guests. In the sixteenth century the lower end of the hall was re-roofed, and a gallery was provided over the cross-passage. It is also possible that at this time the position of the solar and service rooms was transposed. The form finally assumed by the house in the sixteenth century was that of a main block, with three gabled cross-wings facing south-east, and the centre entrance wing recessed as depicted in the Buck print of 1741. Today, there are only two: the north wing containing the present dining room and the de Winton room, and the south wing where the Queen's room is located.

At the dissolution of the priory in 1538, its buildings and lands came, by royal grant, into the possession of Sir John Price (1502?-1555), a member of an old, well-established, Brecknock landed family who became a devoted royal servant but retained a keen interest in the soil. An eminent lawyer, and a renowned classical scholar, he was very critical of the deficiencies of the Welsh clergy, and he attempted to improve matters by publishing in 1546, at his own expense, a kind of instructional manual for their benefit—the first book ever to be published in Welsh. The title-page of the book has been lost, so it is always known by the name *Yny Lhyvyr Hwnn* (In this Book), the initial three words on the first surviving page. Price was very supportive of the policies enshrined in the Acts of Union, 1536-43, because of the benefits which he conceived would ensue for Wales and the Welsh. Royal favour meant that offices fell into his lap like ripe apples, and particularly prestigious and lucrative was the post of secretary to the Council in Wales and the Marches, a position which he held from 1540 until the time of his death. Parliamentary seats came his way also, and he represented Brecknockshire in 1547, Hereford in 1553, and Ludgershall the following year. In 1540 he leased, and in 1542 purchased, the dissolved priory of St Guthlac in a suburb of Hereford, and St Guthlac was to become his principal and greatly beloved home. He died there in 1555, a very wealthy and highly respected man. In his will he was not to forget his home town of Brecon, and certain bequests were made for the benefit of its inhabitants. His possessions there, including Priory House, were left to his second son, Richard. Historian, antiquary, lawyer, humanist scholar, theologian, and successful civil servant, he was all these rolled into one, and when he died at the young age of fifty-three, a truly great light was extinguished.

In the summer of 1645, Priory House, for one night, became a haven of rest for King Charles I. Following his crushing defeat by Oliver Cromwell at Naseby (14 June 1645), Charles had retreated to Cardiff. From there, surrounded by his personal bodyguard, he had ridden over the mountains to Brecon where he found ready sanctuary at the home of Sir Herbert Price, an ardent royalist. Here, weary, disappointed, and dejected, Charles wrote a rather pathetic letter to his eldest son proffering advice on what he should do if ever he found himself in danger of falling into the hands of the victorious parliamentarians. On the following day, Wednesday, 6 August, but not before the inhabitants had given a public display of their loyalty, all the sadder because it was so hollow, the King proceeded to Old Radnor, calling on the way at Gwernyfed, where he dined at the 'fair seat' of Sir Henry Williams. From Old Radnor Charles had pursued his way to Yorkshire before returning to his headquarters at Oxford, which he reached on 28 April 1646.

Sir Herbert Price was succeeded at The Priory by Colonel John Jeffreys, son of Jeffrey Jeffreys and Margaret Price. In 1688, Colonel Jeffreys died, and the priory was inherited by his only surviving child, Dorothy, who later sold it to her kinsman, Sir Jeffrey Jeffreys. His son, Nicholas, was succeeded by two co-heiresses, his wife Frances, and his daughter, Elizabeth, the wife of Charles Pratt, first Earl Camden and Lord Chancellor of England. The steward of the Brecon estate was John Wilkins, and from a letter written by Camden to his daughter, another Elizabeth, it appears that he regarded Wilkins 'to be a rogue'. The house was retained throughout the nineteenth century by the Camdens, who were possessed of substantial property in and around Brecon, and occasionally they were known to stay there. When they were not in residence, the house was leased to members of the local gentry, some of whom were related to the Camdens by marriage. Colonel

Thomas Wood of Gwernyfed, who represented Breconshire in Parliament from 1808-47, lived at the priory for most of that time, and it was he who entertained King George IV at the house in 1821. The king had been returning from Ireland, when a violent storm forced his squadron to seek shelter in Milford Haven. He had then decided to return to London overland, and during his short stay at the priory he had partaken of a magnificent dinner prepared by Mrs Edwards, the wife of Jonathan Edwards, the manager of the recently completed Castle of Brecon Hotel.[8] Following this fine repast, the king had retired to sleep in King Charles's room, 'the great room'. Other prominent families who occupied the house during the century included the Wilkinses, the de Wintons, and the Mayberys. In 1915 Mrs Maybery, daughter of J. R. Cobb, bought the leasehold from Lord Camden. The property had been neglected—in the 1881 census it was listed as uninhabited—and was in need of urgent repair, and this factor was taken into consideration when determining the purchase price.

Priory House: the east gables of the north and south cross-wings

At the beginning of the twentieth century, Mrs Maybery sold the Priory House to her cousin, William Seymour de Winton. A leading lay churchman in Wales, he had been born in the priory in 1856, and had always cherished the ambition of restoring the priory buildings to the church. His dream was now to be realised, and after the creation of the new diocese of Swansea and Brecon in 1923, the Priory House was converted into a deanery and chapter house.

A short run down Priory Hill brings us back to the town, and we can now reflect at leisure on the day's events. Penoyre House is a powerful reminder of 'genteel' living in a glorious rural setting; the Boys' Intermediate School—and the Girls' School was established at the same time—marks the beginning of a golden era in secondary education for the town and its environs; the Priory Church focuses our attention on an age when Brecon was a great religious centre, attracting hordes of pilgrims from all corners of the country; and the Priory House evokes memories of substantial urban gentry, and the extent to which they dominated local Welsh politics and society. Tomorrow we shall concentrate on the town itself, and visit the castle within whose bailey the town really began; the remnants of the town walls with their few surviving towers, and Buckingham Place in Glamorgan Street, where Gwenllian Morgan dwelt.

NOTES

[1] Infra, p. 96-7.

[2] The inn was situated at the junction of Ship Street and Bell Lane. Until recently the premises were occupied by the West Breconshire Farmers' Association. Now it is Harley's Furniture Shop.

[3] Horses had been requisitioned for the war effort.

[4] Infra, p. 97-8.

[5] A form of annuity or pension.

[6] Infra, p. 95-6.

[7] Infra, p. 98.

[8] Sir Charles Morgan of Tredegar Park began work on the site in 1809, and by 1814, after an expenditure of over £7,000, he had transformed what had been the Castle House into the Castle of Brecon Hotel, the first of its kind in Brecon, and one of the earliest in Wales.

Day 5: Brecon Castle, Town Walls and Buckingham Place; Gwenllian Morgan

Today, the car can remain in splendid isolation in the car park, since we can walk comfortably between the places of interest on the day's itinerary. Let us begin with the castle, undoubtedly the oldest building in the ancient borough of Brecon.

The original castle built on the site was constructed by the Norman conqueror of the Kingdom of Brecknock, Bernard de Newmarch. Bernard was a notable warrior knight, and he was the possessor of extensive estates in Herefordshire. Unlike the Romans who built their fortified camp at the Gaer, a few miles to the north-west of Brecon, Bernard appreciated the strategic importance of the spur of land overlooking the rivers Usk and Honddu. On this promontory, in 1093, he built a motte and bailey castle. It was a very substantial fortress as befitted what was to become the *caput* castle of the lordship. Even today, after the erosion of centuries of war, wind and weather the motte, or artificial mound, is still extremely impressive. On this mound Bernard raised a prefabricated wooden tower. Outside the motte was the bailey or courtyard, and at Brecon this was extensive and spade-shaped. It measured about 130 yards in length and nearly 100 yards in width. The bailey would have been defended by a rampart surmounted by a wooden palisade, and on the outside there would have been a further defensive feature in the form of a deep ditch. This was the castle being built by Bernard when the constant and unwelcomed attentions of the Welsh forced him to take the offensive, and he issued forth and defeated the local Welsh chieftain, Bleddyn ap Maenarch, and his overlord, Rhys ap Tewdwr, possibly at Battle. In the history of Brecknock this battle was to prove a decisive turning point. The Norman conqueror now reigned supreme, and his dominance over the lordship, politically and economically, was complete, and was to last until the sixteenth century. It was in the outer ward of this castle, later known as *Beili Glas* (Green Bailey), now defined by Dainter Street, in a little cluster of wooden huts, that a nascent town was to emerge. The original intention had been to extend the town west and north of the

A prospect of Brecon Castle.

castle. The development east of the Honddu appears to have begun almost immediately, and there is no other example on the border where the concurrent development of a town and its castle took place astride a river.[1]

During these early years of conquest, Bernard's hold over his castle and lordship was distinctly precarious. The local Welsh were restless, as they entertained feelings of deep hostility towards a régime which to them was both alien and oppressive. Raid was followed by counter-raid, and in 1094 Bernard was besieged inside his castle until he was relieved by the arrival of Roger de Newburgh. Orchestrating these assaults on the Normans was Gwrgan, Bleddyn's eldest son, who naturally wished to recover what he regarded as being legitimately his. Marauding soldiers ravaged the neighbouring countryside, and people stayed in their houses trembling with fear. Gwrgan was finally captured and placed under house arrest in the castle. On those occasions when he was allowed outside the castle, he was always accompanied by two guards.

Motte and bailey castles in their original form were short-lived. They most certainly met an immediate need, but they were particularly vulnerable to fire. For this reason they were gradually replaced by stone castles though on the original site. Bernard's four grandsons, Roger (d. 1155), Walter (d. 1170), Henry (d. 1175), and Mahel (d. 1175) had all departed this vale of tears without leaving any male heirs, and so, on the death of Mahel, the lordship passed to William de Breos, the husband of Bertha, Bernard's granddaughter and Mahel's younger sister. It is quite possible that it was during William de Breos's tenure of the lordship that the polygonal stone shell keep replaced the wooden tower on the motte. Only three short lengths of the multi-sided shell keep now remain. The wall is almost two yards thick above a battered plinth surrounding an ovoid court some sixteen yards wide. Footings of a fourth side lie beyond a many-sided north-east turret of later date containing a vaulted chamber with one tiny loop.

In the early thirteenth century, in 1217, 1231, and 1233, Brecon and its castle were attacked by Llywelyn ap Iorwerth or Llywelyn Fawr (1173-1240),[2] the prince of Gwynedd. Having consolidated his hold there following the defeat of his uncle, Dafydd I, in 1194, he proceeded to extend his dominion over Perfeddwlad. In 1205 he had married Joan, the daughter of King John. However, good relations with the English Crown were not to be maintained for long despite family ties. In 1211 a royal expedition into Wales saw Llywelyn being deprived of Perfeddwlad. He regained this territory in the following year, and then followed the period of his greatest military successes, for he took advantage of King John's problems with his barons in England, culminating in Magna Carta (1215), to attack the marcher lordships. He succeeded in capturing the key fortresses of Carmarthen, Cardigan, and Montgomery, and was confirmed in these possessions by the Treaty of Worcester, 1218. In the meantime, he had asserted his ascendancy over his fellow princes. His greatest rival among them, Gwenwynwyn, ruler of southern Powys, was exiled in 1216, and his lands were to remain in Llywelyn's custody until the death of the Welsh prince. It was as part of his dynastic ambitions that he attacked Brecon, for he wished to use the lordship as a base for further attacks to the south. In 1217 he placed the town under siege, and it was only after the burgesses had interceded with him, and offered 100 marks and five of their

Brecon Castle from the east.

number as hostages, that he agreed to raise the siege and depart. In 1231 he returned again, but on this occasion he was not to be bought off at any price. The town, though not the castle, was taken and put to the torch, and the prince of Gwynedd 'returned home with great booty'. The same fate awaited the town the following year when Llywelyn, taking advantage of Henry III's difficulties in England with the barons, led by Richard Marshall, made his fiercest onslaught yet on Brecon castle, investing it for a whole month with the most up-to-date machinery of siege warfare. It was all to no avail; the castle proved impregnable and Llywelyn, totally frustrated, withdrew to the north, but not before consigning the little settlement at the foot of the castle, with its dwellings probably built of timber, to the all-devouring flame to the utter despair of the burgesses cowering within the castle walls. But the town, phoenix-like, rose from the ashes again.

In 1241 Eleanor, the heir of the de Breos family, married one of the de Bohuns. It was about this time that stone walls were built to encompass the bailey, a development which had become very necessary following successive assaults by the Welsh. The hall, the south wall of which still survives, was probably erected in the 1270s, and this was the period which witnessed the greatest development of the castle.

By the 1250s baronial opposition to the King had come to a head under the leadership of Simon de Montfort, who was supported also by prominent marcher lords like the lord of Brecon. It soon developed into actual hostilities along the border, where the Mortimer lands were raided by the rebels, among whom was Humphrey de Bohun at the head of his Brecon followers. Prince Edward, the King's heir, now came to the border to save Mortimer. He invaded the Bohun territories, taking the three castles of Huntington, Hay and Brecon, which were then entrusted to Roger Mortimer.

At this time, also, Brecon figured prominently in the schemes of Llywelyn ap Gruffydd, the grandson of Llywelyn Fawr, to unite Wales. For him, Brecon was a very useful launching pad from which to attack Gilbert de Clare, lord of Glamorgan, thus enabling his hegemony to be extended to the Bristol Channel. It was for this reason that in 1273 he besieged Humphrey de Bohun VII in his castle at Brecon. The threat posed by Llywelyn was only finally to be removed following, first, his defeat by Edward I in 1277, and secondly, his death at the hands of Stephen de Frankton at Cilmery in 1282.

In 1322 Brecon castle became a royal stronghold. On the death of Humphrey de Bohun VII in 1299, his son, Humphrey de Bohun VIII, succeeded to the family possessions. He promptly showed himself to be a true member of the Bohun family by joining the barons in their opposition to the Crown. However, in 1322, a punitive expedition was dispatched by Edward II against the marcher lords. The campaign was short and sharp, and the castles of Clifford, Hay, Bronllys, and later, Penkelly and Brecon, were captured. The lordship of Brecon now became a royal possession, and, following this success, the King returned home by way of Crickhowell, Abergavenny, and Gloucester. After the fall of Brecon castle, its lord, de Bohun, went north to join the leader of the dissident nobles, Thomas Lancaster, Lord Clifford, who was advancing south to intercept the King. On 16 March, at Boroughbridge, the baronial levies were defeated, and amongst the slain was the lord of Brecon.

Humphrey de Bohun's son, John, was a minor and, until 1326, when he attained his majority, the Brecon lands were in the wardship of Hugh le Despenser. Between 1326-73 the lordship of Brecon was retained by the de Bohuns, after which it passed, via an heiress, Mary, the daughter of Humphrey de Bohun X, into the hands of Henry Bolingbroke, Duke of Lancaster—who ruled as Henry IV, 1399-1413—and his descendants. It was during Henry's reign that a major insurrection took place in Wales which was to threaten the very existence of both castle and town. The revolt of Owain Glyndŵr soon attained national proportions, and the plantation towns of Wales were prime targets for his followers. Brecon was of particular significance since, as a royal stronghold, it assisted the English government to maintain its hold over the country, however precarious. No sooner had the rebellion broken out than John Leventhorpe, the receiver-general of the Duchy of Lancaster, was busily organising the defences of the castle. In July

1402 Richard, Lord Grey of Codnor, was placed in charge of the defences, and a force of forty men-at-arms and two hundred archers was placed at his disposal, each man-at-arms receiving 12*d*. per day and each bowman 6*d*. The castle walls were repaired at considerable expense, and the most up-to-date instruments of warfare—cannons, gunpowder, saltpetre, and sulphur—were stored there. The military commander assumed full control of both judicial and civil administration, and Brecon, at a moment of grave crisis, was, in effect, placed under martial law and remained in that state for the duration of the hostilities. The town was also placed on full alert and its defences strengthened, and a grant of 100 marks (£66 13*s*. 4*d*.) was made by the government towards that end, though it was understood that the burgesses were expected to raise a similar amount. For the purpose of manning the town walls, the burgesses were organised into a kind of home-guard. These measures were not undertaken a minute too soon, for the castle and town were besieged on several occasions, but the defences were never breached. However, together with the resolution of the defenders, external factors played a major part in the survival of both castle and town. On Sunday 1 July 1403, they were only saved by the timely arrival of a relief force led by John Bodenham, the sheriff of Herefordshire. He scattered the besiegers, leaving some 240 of them dead; and in the autumn the news of a royal expedition moving down the Usk valley was sufficient to put the rebels to flight. The insurgents were anything but persistent.

In 1429 the lordship was acquired by Anne, Countess of Stafford, the granddaughter of Mary of Bohun, and she was succeeded by her son, Humphrey, Duke of Buckingham (1439-60), 'a most miserable covetous grinding man that mightily oppressed the country'. Apart from a brief spell in 1483-5, the lordship then remained in the hands of the Buckingham family until the attainder and execution of the last Duke in 1521, when the lands escheated to the crown.

Following the death of Humphrey at the battle of Northampton in 1460, Brecknock passed to his son, Henry, a minor. The wardship was given to Anne, Duchess of Exeter, the king's sister, but the stewardship of the castle and lordship was bestowed on Sir William Herbert, the first Earl of Pembroke. Buckingham, in due course, became a powerful henchman of Richard of Gloucester, and assisted him in his ambitious and dangerous designs to usurp the crown. He became the recipient of the loaves and fishes from a grateful royal hand, and Buckingham, as a result, became one of the greatest of the 'overmighty' subjects. Together with the lordship of Brecon, he was governor of the King's castles in Wales, steward of all the royal manors in Shropshire and Hereford, Chief Justice and Chamberlain of both north and south Wales, and Lord High Constable of England. Furthermore, he had royal blood in his veins since, on his father's side, he was descended from Anne, daughter of Thomas Woodstock, the fifth son of Edward III, while on his mother's side he was descended from John Beaufort, son of John of Gaunt. And, despite his support of Richard, he had good Lancastrian credentials as well, since his father, and both his grandfathers, had suffered death in battle fighting for the Red Rose. Buckingham, indeed, cast a very long shadow over the throne.

It was such a man, powerful in his own right, and close to the throne, that Richard chose to alienate in 1483. He insulted him in words, and delayed granting Buckingham offices and lands to which the latter considered himself entitled. The death of the two young princes, the sons of Edward IV, in most suspicious circumstances in the Tower, was the last straw. Buckingham now decided to throw in his lot with Henry Tudor and, at Brecon Castle, he and Bishop Morton of Ely, a prisoner whom Richard had committed to his charge, hatched a plot to overthrow the King and place Henry on the throne. The outlines of the conspiracy are clear enough. While Buckingham created a diversion at home by staging a rebellion, Henry was to invade the country from abroad. However, fickle fate in the form of perverse nature, now took a hand, for while a storm in the English Channel forced Henry's squadron to return to harbour in France, the same tempest caused the river Severn to flood thus preventing Buckingham's levies from proceeding any further eastwards. His troops, unpaid and mutinous, gradually melted away. Shortly afterwards, Buckingham himself was betrayed, and executed without trial at Salisbury by Richard, who then confiscated his estates.

Buckingham's absence from his lordship provided Sir Thomas Vaughan and his brothers of Tretower, ardent Yorkists, with a glorious opportunity which they seized eagerly. They now attacked, captured and plundered Brecon Castle, Buckingham's base. It was all to no avail, because on 22 August 1485, at Bosworth, the Lancastrian Henry Tudor met and defeated Richard III. Henry then ascended the English throne as King Henry VII, and he was to be the first of a line of illustrious Tudor monarchs. But the Vaughans of Tretower were not finished with dissent yet, and in 1486 Brecon became the scene of another conspiracy. Assisted by the Herberts, Sir Thomas Vaughan now let loose the dogs of war there, and raised a rebellion aimed at overthrowing the new sovereign. Their attempt to seize Brecon castle failed, as its garrison of 140 soldiers successfully withstood a siege of seven weeks' duration, for which they received £48 in wages. The insurrection was finally suppressed by Sir Rhys ap Thomas, undoubtedly Henry's strongest pillar of support in south Wales.

The damage sustained by the fabric of the castle from these twin attacks must have been considerable, for in 1500 the Council of Edward, Duke of Buckingham, to whom the family estates had been restored following Henry VII's triumph, found it necessary to undertake extensive repairs in order to make it habitable. The buildings needed to be weather-proofed, and the Council arranged for the retiling of the roof, and the replacing of its lead, which had been stripped off because it was so valuable. The work must have been performed satisfactorily, for in 1521 the King's surveyors, Thomas Magnus and William Walweyn, reported that the castle was 'a good and a stronghold, with all the houses of offices and lodgings builded after the old fashion; except there is a goodly hall set on height, only with lights in either end, and none upon the sides'. The hall had also been provided with a new roof at considerable expense 'with pendants after a goodly fashion'. From this valuation it also appears that water for the castle was supplied from a conduit. The domestic apartments thus made good probably comprised the kitchen, pantry, buttery, cellars, bakehouse, brewhouse, solars or private chambers, the nursery, and possibly even a study.

When John Leland, as part of his celebrated itinerary of Henry VIII's Kingdom, visited Brecon in the 1540s, he described the castle as standing in the suburbs, and divided from the town by the river Honddu which was spanned by a high bridge with two arches. He then continues: 'the castle is very large, strong, well maintained; and the keep of the castle is very large and fair'. However, in 1609, a 'Certificate of his Majesty's decayed Castles' depicts the castle at Brecon as 'decayed saving the great hall in which the Justice of Assise do sit'. But despite the decline, John Speed's excellent map of the town in 1610 shows the castle's *enceinte* to be still intact.

In 1534 Bishop Rowland Lee, the President of the Council in Wales and the Marches, had been particularly desirous that money should be spent on necessary repairs to Brecon castle. His anxiety had arisen from the danger of revolt which had followed in the wake of Henry VIII's breach with Rome and the dissolution of the religious houses. This policy had had the effect of alienating conservative opinion within the country, and the rebels could expect support from Catholic Europe. In the event neither the insurrection nor the invasion took place, but it was a scenario which Lee could ill afford to ignore.

It would appear that shortly after the death of Elizabeth I in 1603, the castle, which had successfully withstood repeated assaults by the Welsh during the Middle Ages, was once again threatened with destruction by them. Thomas Powell, the poet who recounted this tale in Welsh doggerel while languishing in gaol in 1680, declared that 1,200 local Welshmen, incensed by the tyrannical and oppressive manner of collecting the annual rents, marched on the castle armed with billhooks and threatened to reduce it to the condition of Troy, and drag the governor, Henry Vaughan of Moccas, the lieutenant and steward of Brecknock, 'bleeding from his chamber'. Vaughan, however, stood firm and the rebels, dispirited by their lack of success, retreated bootless to the hills from whence they had originally come.

In the autumn of 1645, shortly after the departure of Charles I from Brecon on 6 August 1645, Major-General Rowland Laugharne, a young and energetic parliamentary commander, at the invitation of those local gentry who were well-disposed towards Parliament, arrived at the town to an enthusiastic reception. The royalists were penned up inside the castle, whose defences were organised by Colonel Turberville Morgan. Laugharne beset the castle and, after a short siege, the defenders surrendered. The parliamentary troops then slighted the defences, and pursued this kind of destruction of royalist strongholds all over Wales.

Hall block, Brecon Castle.

However, Brecon castle was more than a bastion of defence against the potentially insurgent Welsh outside its walls; it was also the administrative centre of a very substantial lordship. Located within it was the exchequer, which handled revenue—moneys collected and rendered by local officials. By the fourteenth century the total collected amounted to the not inconsiderable sum of £1,000 a year from rents and other dues. It also housed the chancery, where the register of writs was kept; there, too, were held the lord's courts like the Great Sessions and the manorial courts. The manorial courts, the Courts Baron[3] and Leet,[4] met at *Beili Glas*, and it was at the Court Leet, at least until 1556, that view of frankpledge was held, and the constables for the twelve wards of the town appointed. Furthermore, in the castle was to be found the county gaol, certainly until 1690, when it was replaced by another jail built in the Watton which, according to Hugh Thomas, the Breconshire Herald, was as big, strong, and handsome 'as any on this side England or Wales'. Situated there, also, was the armoury and, to cater for the spiritual needs of the garrison, nestling within the protective ramparts, lay the little chapel of St Nicholas, the patron saint of children and sailors. But the lord in his castle, in theory at least, regulated as well all forms of commercial activity within his domains, so that he might be persuaded, for financial or other considerations, to confer important economic and civic privileges on the burgesses residing in the town. Hence the numerous charters granted to it by successive lords throughout the Middle Ages.[5] The cumulative effect of all these grants was, that by the early sixteenth century, the town was possessed of complete self-government.

Together with being a defensive base and an administrative centre, the castle was also home to the lords of Brecon when they chose to visit their lordship. Though they were not normally resident in the castle because conditions in a border zone were far too hazardous to make living there an attractive proposition—the de Bohuns were particularly lax in this respect in the fourteenth century—there were occasions when, with their retinues, they did reside there, and some of these stays could be quite protracted. The lord's sojourn at the castle might be occasioned by defensive considerations, or as a prelude to a military expedition. On the other hand, it might be part and parcel of a grand progress which the lord was undertaking of his estates. In the 1270s Humphrey de Bohun wrested control of Brecon from Llywelyn ap Gruffydd in a spirited and daring campaign, while in 1397 Henry Bolingbroke came to Brecon as part of a peaceful progress which he was making of his vast estates. One lord, Humphrey de Bohun X (1361-77), made Brecon castle his principal residence, and for that reason he had the castle greatly extended and beautified at his own expense. The last of the feudal lords of Brecon, Edward Stafford, Duke of Buckingham, who was executed in 1521, partly because of the King's suspicions of his ambitions, and partly on account of the implacable hostility of Cardinal Thomas Wolsey, Henry VIII's chief minister, was even born at the castle on 3 February 1477.

The most impressive features of the castle today are the south wall of the hall block and the Ely tower. The hall is two storeys high with low cellars beneath. The wall now is some twenty-three yards long and two and a half yards wide, and ends in the east in a round tower against which abuts a slightly later, semi-polygonal latrine turret. The outer perimeter wall with its gateways and towers, as depicted in the Buck brothers' engraving, though these did not appear in Meredith Jones's plan of 1744, have all disappeared. The dressed stone, undoubtedly, was used by the townspeople for building purposes.

In the mind's eye one can conjure up quick snapshots of some aspects of the castle's past history: the frenetic activity and noise that accompanied its construction; the wild shouts of Welsh tribesmen as they assailed its walls, and their screams of anguish as they fell dying at their base; the holding of the courts and the pronouncement of judgements; the delivery of moneys and the auditing of accounts; the merriment in the great hall when guests were entertained in sumptuous style, and the splendour and pageantry when the lord and his family, accompanied by a numerous train, paid a visit. But the fortress could also be a grim and forbidding place with prisoners dying of disease in its ill-lit and filthy dungeon, and bleeding, headless corpses dangling by their ankles from the walls. Furthermore, the castle was home to dark conspiracies with plans being laid to topple monarchs. If only the walls could give utterance to all that they have seen and heard; what startling revelations would follow, and what a profound experience that would be.

Having examined closely the defences of the castle, it is now time to establish the nature of the protection which was afforded the little town that sprang up with mushroom rapidity to the east of the Honddu. After all, this settlement, peopled initially by craftsmen and their families attracted from Hereford, was situated in a border zone where conditions in the Middle Ages were very unsettled and even dangerous. The townspeople had to be assured of some degree of security for life and limb, otherwise the prospect of living there would have been too uninviting. Furthermore, it was most desirable that the castle should be provided with a second line of defence, and so, during the thirteenth century, the town came to be encompassed by a strong stone wall, served by four major gates, the line of which is still fairly clear.

This defensive barrier was oval in shape, and about 1066 yards in length, which must have made it very difficult to defend against a determined foe. It ran from a drawbridge outside the postern gate of the castle to the Struet Gate in the north. From there it passed through a field known as *Clawdd y Gaer,* running behind and roughly parallel with Lion Street, to the Watton gate in the east. From here, the wall curved round to the Usk, along the line of Captain's Walk, and then followed the course of the river to two gates in the west, in close proximity to each other, known as Bridge gate and Water gate. The former led to the bridge, described by the Breconshire Herald, Hugh Thomas, in 1698 as one of the fairest in the kingdom and supported by seven arches, which spanned the Usk at this point, while the latter opened out on another bridge, built on three arches, which crossed the Honddu. The wall then continued along this river to link up again with the drawbridge. On the inner side of the wall was a raised walk, from which defenders could discharge missles at assailing forces while being afforded protection for themselves by a parapet. To make life even more hazardous and difficult for the enemy, outside the wall, on the landward side, was a deep fosse, or ditch, filled with water from a stream flowing down Cerrig Cochion hill. The wall was provided with additional strength by the presence of ten towers, placed equidistantly apart, some of which were rectangular in shape, while others were D-shaped. For the maintenance and repair of these walls grants of murage were made to the corporation, though Henry IV granted to the burgesses exemption from the payment of this toll. In 1404, when the town was threatened by the forces of Owain Glyndŵr, the walls were extensively repaired, and much later in the century, in 1483, during the abortive attempt by Buckingham and Bishop Morton to overthrow Richard III, £10 were spent on further repairs to it. The revolt was a timely reminder to Richard, if he ever needed reminding, of the fragility of his position on the throne, and the real threat posed by Henry Tudor. He now proceeded to buttress his position in south Wales by placing local supporters in key positions—in the lordship of Brecknock he increasingly relied on the Vaughan family of Tretower—and strengthening strongholds in his possession. One such fortress which had recently come into his hands following the execution of Henry, Duke of Buckingham, the price of failure in 1483, was Brecon, and £60 were now spent on reinforcing the town walls. But together with its defensive value, and a deterrent to potential enemies, the presence of a strong stone wall was also a matter of prestige, since such a wall was symbolic of the town's status, its degree of prosperity, and its spirit of independence and civic pride.

John Speed's map of Brecon is most useful not only for its depiction of the castle, but also because it delineates the line of the town wall and the relative position of its gates and towers. In Speed's estimate, the town walls in 1610 'were strong and of good repair'. By mid-century the situation had changed dramatically. Relations between the early Stuart monarchs, James I (1603-25), and Charles I (1625-49), and their Parliaments, had steadily deteriorated, and in 1642 matters had reached such a pass that the inevitable consequence was civil war. Even though Brecon town, and the majority of the local gentry, had declared for the King, the loyalty was only skin deep, and the ambivalent attitude of the worthy citizens of Brecon was made abundantly clear when they embarked upon the destruction of the town walls. This act was intended to relieve them of the expense of maintaining a garrison, and it also meant that they would not have to place in jeopardy their own lives by being summoned to help man its ramparts. Doubtless, there would have been a realisation, too, of the futility of defending walls, however sturdy, against parliamentary cannon. For the burgesses, the preservation of their town with its numerous trades was of far greater importance than the upholding of the majesty of a distant monarch. The destruction of the walls was not wholesale, as Hugh Thomas, at the close of the century, described them as being in 'indifferent good repair'. It was only in 1785 that the gates were destroyed.

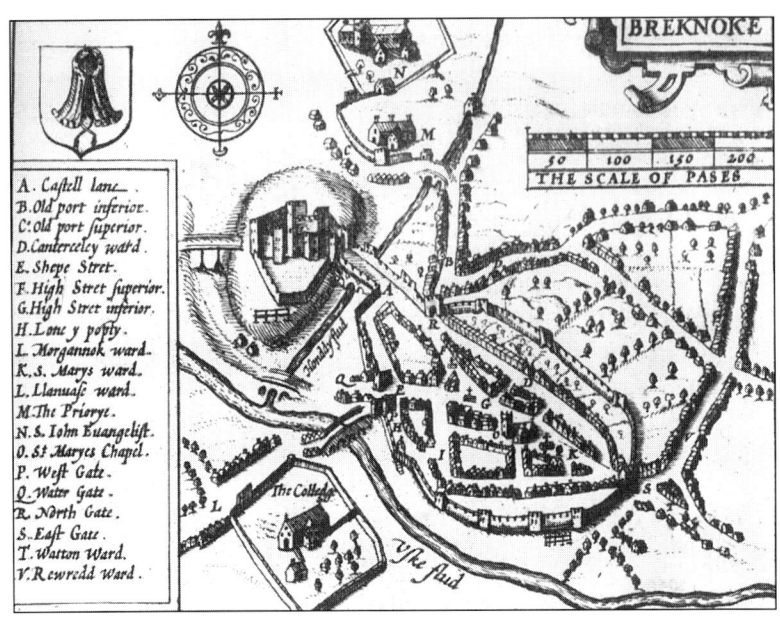

John Speed's map of Brecon, 1610.

A section of the town hall by Captain's Walk.

114

Short stretches of the town wall, together with a few towers, are still visible. In the town car park, and behind McCartneys, Auctioneers, Surveyors, and Estate Agents, there is a length of wall together with a rectangular tower. From the car park we can enter Free Street, and located on a considerable mound to the rear of the Inland Revenue Office is another stretch of wall and another tower. It is a comparatively easy matter then to proceed from Free Street, past the Brecknock Museum, to Captain's Walk towards the end of which another length of wall and a tower have survived. All vestiges of the town ditch, however, have totally disappeared, completely filled in by the débris of centuries.

From Captain's Walk it is only a short stroll along Glamorgan Street to Buckingham Place, an imposing urban dwelling dating from the mid-sixteenth and early seventeenth centuries, and home to many of the town's most noteworthy citizens.

This large stone building has been subjected to so many alterations over the centuries that it is now difficult to establish the nature of the original plan. The datable features of the house would suggest two main periods in its construction before the outbreak of the Civil War in 1642: the mid-sixteenth century block embracing the west end of the main range, while the remainder of the main range belongs to the early seventeenth century. The dwelling probably conformed to the end hall plan with a cross passage, though the hall would not have been open to the roof in the usual medieval fashion, but would have had another storey above it. Beyond the cross passage there would have been the service rooms and the kitchen. Apart from the main range measuring about 87 feet by 26 feet, there is a subsidiary building to the north-west of it, the two being joined by a short connecting block, of which no original work now remains. Though it is tempting to regard this building as a banqueting house, this interpretation has to be abandoned for two reasons: first, banqueting houses were usually built of timber, and secondly, they would appear to have been completely detached structures set at a distance from the house. Since this building is attached to the main block, it is safer to postulate that it was a 'parlour' wing, though the lack of an original fireplace and chimney stack does present problems. What is certain is that Buckingham Place was the residence of a very wealthy, and most important, local gentleman. If the house is not earlier than mid-sixteenth century, this discounts the theory that it belonged to the last Duke of Buckingham because he was beheaded in 1521. Tradition has it that his ghost may still be seen at midnight flitting through his former residence. In any case he was born at the castle which was not too far distant and why, consequently, should he have built another home for himself in the town?

Buckingham Place, Brecon.

Another theory which has been advanced, and Gwenllian Morgan was one of the proponents of this view, is that Buckingham Place was built by a Dr Awbrey of Abercynrig in the reign of Elizabeth I. The poet, Thomas Churchyard (1520-1604), speaking of Brecon, declared that 'Dr Awberie hath a house there', and it is an established fact that it was a great-great-great grandson of this Dr Awbrey who, having fallen on bad times, sold it in the seventeenth century to William Morgan of Y Dderw, Llyswen, a member of the

Tredegar family. He, in turn, had leased the property to Dr William Lucy, Bishop of St David's (1660-77), the Bishop's Palace at St David's being then largely a ruin, and the house continued to be the official residence of the bishops of the diocese throughout the latter half of the seventeenth century. It was important for the bishops of St David's to have a dwelling in Brecon since, after all, it was the largest town in the eastern half of their vast diocese.

In the latter half of the sixteenth century, a possible early occupant of the newly-built house was Meredith Thomas. During the twenty years extending from 1564-84, he occupied the prestigious office of bailiff on no fewer than eight occasions. He was a lawyer, a notary public and deputy registrar of the archdeaconry of Brecon, and his will demonstrates not only that he lived in Glamorgan Street, but that he was also a man of considerable substance. Thus, he was possessed of another dwelling in Cantref Selyf ward, together with barns, stables, backsides,[6] kilns, and breweries. He further owned barns, orchards, and gardens in the Watton, and a meadow called 'Lack Issa' where he grazed four oxen, nineteen kine, fourteen young cattle, and 240 sheep. From this it is quite evident that townsmen like Meredith Thomas were countrymen at heart.

From the Tredegar family the house passed in the eighteenth century to the banker, Jeffreys Wilkins, who later sold it to his nephew, Thomas Maybery, a solicitor in the town, and prothonotary of the Brecknock Circuit. Maybery divided the dwelling into three houses, and it was during these alterations, which included an additional wing to one end, that a large stone was found beneath the wainscot above a former fireplace with the Awbrey arms sculptured upon it. Unfortunately, this crucial bit of evidence has since been lost. At various times in the nineteenth century Buckingham Place has been the residence of the Earl of Brecknock, and of Howel Gwyn, Conservative, and Cyril Flower, Liberal, when they represented Brecon in Parliament. From 1868-1939 it was home, also, to Gwenllian Morgan, a great champion of women's rights, who became the first woman to hold office as a councillor and as a mayor in Brecon and, for that matter, in Wales as a whole.

117

Gwenllian Elizabeth Fanny Morgan, later to be affectionately known as Miss Philip Morgan, was born on 9 April 1852 at Penpentre, Defynnog where her ancestors had held land and property for over three hundred years. She was one of four children, two of whom, a boy and a girl, had died in infancy. Her father, Philip Morgan, was perpetual curate of Pen-pont (1841-64), and of Battle (1859-64), and afterwards, from 1864 until his death in 1868, rector of Llanhamlach. The mother was Margaret, daughter of William Hughes of Llanfaes, Brecon, and The Parc, Trallong. When their uncle, the Rev. William Hughes, J.P., of Ebbw Vale, died, Gwenllian Morgan and her sister Ellen (Nellie) inherited the maternal grandmother's estate which included The Parc.

Whereas today women enjoy equal rights with men, it was not always so, and it was very largely through the dogged determination of women like Gwenllian Morgan that they achieved emancipation from the thraldom which, for so many, was a feature of their humdrum lives. When she was born, women were servile, and in Queen Victoria's reign (1837-1901) men shared T. H. Huxley's view that the female was subordinate to man, and it is hardly surprising to discover, therefore, that women were often mistreated by their husbands, a situation that applied even to the wives of the well-to-do.

Life for girls from working-class backgrounds was particularly hard. Until the passing of the Mines Act in 1842, they could be found hauling coal underground, or carrying it to the surface in baskets strapped to their backs. Others, and these were the ones that laboured hardest of all, worked as seamstresses in 'Sweat Shops', and so harsh were the conditions of work that they were known to lose their sight. Still more were employed in the woollen mills and factories, and if they were unfortunate enough to suffer injury during the course of their employment, there was no compensation available. But the occupation which engaged the majority of young girls, and one that was also very demanding, was that of housemaid, on farms and in private dwellings. The working day of these housemaids was exceedingly long, extending from 6 a.m. to 10 p.m. with a break of half an hour for breakfast, an hour for lunch, and half an hour each for tea and supper. The employment could also be exhausting, as it involved carrying coal and water, making beds, filling and emptying baths, and the like. Since many of the working women were mothers as well, during their absence in the day the babies had to be cared for by the eldest child, a situation that was highly unsatisfactory.

Apart from their conditions of work, women suffered under other grave disadvantages. It was generally felt that girls should not be presented with the same educational opportunities as the boys. They were not candidates for higher education, and there was no room for them in the universities, or in professions like the law and medicine. Furthermore, women took no part in administration either at local level as councillors, or at national level as members of Parliament, and they did not enjoy the right to vote. Though the opportunities for education for girls from working-class homes were severely limited, those from wealthier ones were more fortunate because they could attend a private school, or be educated at home by a family tutor. But even for these girls the study of mathematics and science caused raised eyebrows; to their parents the purpose of education was to prepare girls for marriage to successful men. One mother remarked that a girl could not be sent to the kitchen reciting the multiplication table. When University College, Cardiff, was established in 1883, it was the first mixed college in Wales, and though the earliest of the Welsh University Colleges, Aberystwyth, had been founded in 1872, it was not until 1884 that it admitted a woman student. It was only in 1870 that a Welsh woman gained her M.D., and then it was in Zürich rather than in London, the capital's medical schools being closed to people of her gender. The lady in question was Frances Elizabeth Hoggan, and she had been born in Brecon on 20 December 1843, the daughter of Richard Morgan, curate of St John's. Arising from the vigorous campaign waged by the suffragettes, and the contribution made by women, including the suffragettes, to the war effort after 1914, Lloyd George's Coalition government in 1918 conferred the vote on women over thirty, providing they were householders, or married to house-holders, and in 1919 Nancy Astor proudly took her seat in Parliament, the first woman to be so honoured. Ten years later, in 1928, Baldwin's Conservative government enfranchised women over twenty-one. It was now quite apparent that the tide could not be turned; a brave new world of opportunity was opening for women.

An old well-established Welsh family, the Morgans boasted a pedigree which extended back to Brychan, prince of Brycheiniog, and the pride in their lineage was reflected in the family motto, *Gwell angau na chywilydd* (Better death than dishonour). Though Welsh society, religiously, in the nineteenth century, was split between *capel a llan* (chapel and church), the Morgans had a foot in each camp as they were generous in their financial support of both the established church and the Nonconformist denominations. However, their chief loyalty, undoubtedly, was to the Anglican communion. Not only was Gwenllian Morgan's father a clergyman, so, too, was her uncle, William Hughes. Another colourful member of the family was the Rev. Thomas Morgan, D.D., R.N., who was educated at Christ College, Brecon, and Wadham College, Oxford. He became chaplain of H.M.S. *Alfred* in 1793, and his avowed intention was to avenge the execution of Louis XVI that same year by the French revolutionaries. It must, therefore, have been most satisfying to him to have taken part in 1794 in the engagement known as the 'Glorious First of June' when Lord Howe inflicted a crushing defeat on the French fleet off Ushant. Another noteworthy member of the family was William Philips who became town clerk of Brecon in 1678, and later, in 1689, bailiff. An eminent scholar and antiquarian, the preservation of the Brecon charters is very largely due to him as, in 1679, he laboriously copied them by hand into an old register of the borough. Captain Thomas Philips was another relation, and he it was who gave his name to Captain's Walk, which lay below the town wall at the bottom of his garden in Glamorgan Street. This walk was much improved later by the French prisoners taken during the Napoleonic War.

The Rev. Philip Morgan died at Defynnog in 1868, and his widow then took her two daughters to live at No 2, Buckingham Place, Brecon. The mother died in February 1884, and Nellie then undertook the running of the household, an arrangement which enabled her elder sister to devote time and energy to her manifold outside activities and interests.

A subject close to her heart was the welfare of the poor. While she had little patience with shirkers, she had a genuine sympathy for those who were down on their luck. Though she came from a wealthy family, she well understood the daily hardships that others had to suffer through poverty, and she provided what support she could. She appreciated the distress caused to workers and their families by 'lay-offs' when labourers were sent home because adverse weather conditions precluded the possibility of their working, and during these periods they were not paid. This was an age when there was no National Assistance or unemployment benefit and, being proud men, they loathed the idea of being dependent on parish relief. To those that were sick, to the elderly ladies in the almshouses, and to children in the workhouse, she gave special attention. Her services were given willingly to practically every branch of social work in the county of Brecon, serving on committees, and often acting as president. Education was of special interest to her, and she served as a member of the Breconshire Education Committee, and became a governor of the two Brecon County Schools. Her commitment to the welfare of the underdog saw her appointed a Poor Law Guardian in 1894. Gwenllian Morgan also actively supported the temperance movement, and she rendered invaluable assistance to her friend, Lady Henry Somerset, a tireless worker in the cause. Both ladies appreciated the unfortunate consequences that could stem from the worship of Bacchus, among them degradation and poverty. It was a vicious circle, really, because poverty could lead to intemperance, and intemperance, in turn, could intensify poverty. Inns or 'pubs' were a conspicuous feature of townscapes in the nineteenth century, and they were to be found in abundance in rural areas as well; they provided relief, even temporary oblivion, from the wretchedness and misery which daily dogged the very footsteps of workmen. The numerous inns of Brecon—in the 1830s there were some forty-seven watering holes in the town—must have been a cause of considerable concern to both ladies. But other worthy causes received her attention. Thus she was a member of the Welsh Advisory Committee, chairwoman of the Breconshire Association of Friendly Societies, a member of the County Insurance Committee and, when war broke out in 1914, she became the first president of the Brecon Ladies' Working Party.

Miss Gwenllian Morgan, Mayor of Brecon, 1910-11.

In politics, Gwenllian Morgan was a liberal, and she became a close friend of Cyril Flower and his wife, Constance, of Aston Clinton, Tring, Herts. Constance Flower was the daughter of the great philanthropist and educationist, Lady de Rothschild. Her husband, Cyril, represented Brecon town in Parliament from 1880-5, and he was the last to do so since, as a result of the Parliamentary Reform Act of 1884, the borough—together with Llywel—lost the right to return its own representative to the House of Commons. Cyril Flower was later elevated to the peerage, taking the title of Lord Battersea.

At the beginning of the nineteenth century, as women were now eligible to stand for local government, and in response to a letter signed by people of all classes and shades of opinion in Brecon requesting her to put her name forward, Gwenllian Morgan agreed to fight for a seat on Brecon Borough Council. She was duly elected, and thus became the first woman in Wales to serve in that capacity. In 1910 she was again a candidate, and the electors demonstrated their confidence in this champion of women's rights by returning her with a substantial majority of 110 votes. In this year she passed another milestone because, despite the objections and misgivings of many male councillors, she was elected mayor, and became the first woman in the Principality to achieve this distinction. One of those who objected strongly to her elevation to the position of mayor was Councillor C. W. Bert. He gave it as his opinion—and Gwenllian Morgan respected his view—that the 'advancement of women to such positions was not to the advantage of the community or to the advantage of womanhood itself'. 1910-11 was an important year for the first woman mayor of Brecon, since it was Coronation Year, the new King, George V, being crowned at Westminster Abbey on 22 June 1911. It would appear that Gwenllian Morgan performed her numerous duties as mayor with conspicuous dignity and grace. She did not attend the coronation preferring to remain at home to organise the celebrations there, and providing entertainment especially for the children. However, she was present at Caernarvon Castle on 13 July 1911 on the occasion of the Investiture of the Prince of Wales, and her appearance in the procession in full mayoral regalia was greeted with a great cheer from the assembled throng. In 1912, in the Guild Hall, Brecon, in recognition of her high character, exceptional accomplishments, and dedicated public service, Gwenllian Morgan was presented with a portrait of herself, painted in oils by John Cooke of Chelsea, and an illuminated address, the total cost being borne by almost a thousand female subscribers, no man being permitted to contribute. Gwenllian Morgan was to continue to sit on the council until 1923, by which time she was seventy-one years old.

A lady endowed with considerable intellectual gifts, Gwenllian Morgan was an eloquent public speaker with a commendable command of the English language. Allied to her ability in public affairs, particularly those relating to education and the care of the poor, she demonstrated a considerable interest in the history and antiquities of her native county. She was an avid researcher, and in her house was a fine collection of prints, manuscripts, and engravings.

A regular contributor to the antiquarian journals edited by W. R. Williams of Tal-y-bont, she was an ardent admirer of Theophilus Jones, and she wrote a biographical study of him which was included in the volume, *Theophilus Jones, Historian*. Her labours in this particular vineyard received due recognition in 1935 when she was elected a Fellow of the Society of Antiquarians. However, her major interest was in the Silurist, Henry Vaughan. She uncovered many facts concerning his early life and when, in 1895, she met the American, Louise Imogen Guiney (1861-1920), another 'specialist' on Vaughan, they agreed to bring out a joint edition of the poet's works, with biographical and historical notes. The project was announced as early as 1896, but the two friends died without completing it. Their large collections were handed over in 1930 to Dr F. E. Hutchinson, who used them for his standard book, *Henry Vaughan* (1947).

Throughout her life, despite her civic, educational and antiquarian interests, Gwenllian Morgan's devotion to the Priory Church of St John the Evangelist, later, after 1923, to become the Cathedral Church of the newly created diocese of Swansea and Brecon, never waned. She was church-warden between 1920-22, and her considerable knowledge of the fabric enabled her to deliver informed lectures, pen valuable articles, including a history of the Havard Chapel, and to produce a guide book, the first edition of which appeared in 1903 and the fourteenth in 1961.

On 21 July 1925 the University of Wales conferred on Gwenllian Morgan the honorary degree of M.A. (*Magister in Artibus*) in recognition of her researches into the life and works of Henry Vaughan, and for being a 'pioneer in the emancipation of women from matters of a purely domestic nature'. Professor Mary Williams, who introduced the graduand, concluded her address by declaring, 'The University of Wales honours itself by including among its graduates the name of Miss Gwenllian Morgan'.

Towards the end of her life this remarkable woman suffered a great deal from ill-health. Her appearances in the streets of the ancient borough, always accompanied by her red dachshund and a fawn pug, became increasingly rare, though she still welcomed people to her home. She died there on 7 November 1939, aged eighty-seven. In accordance with her wishes, her body was cremated, and the ashes placed in her sister's grave (Nellie had died in August 1926) at Pen-pont. A suitable epitaph for Gwenllian Morgan can surely be found in the words uttered at the time of her death by the then mayor of Brecon, Councillor William Williams. For him, 'A great light had been extinguished'. In conclusion, it is appropriate to say that, together with the other 'greats' of Brecon, worthies like Sarah Siddons, Thomas Coke and Theophilus Jones, Gwenllian Elizabeth Fanny Morgan has left her own indelible footprint in the sands of time.

It is time now to return to our hotel and refresh ourselves. Tomorrow will be our final day in this ancient borough and its environs, when another door will be opened to reveal even more about the town's mesmeric past.

NOTES

[1] I am indebted to Peter White Esq., of the Royal Commission on the Ancient and Historical Monuments of Wales, for this information.

[2] The Great.

[3] The assembly of freehold tenants of a manor under the lord.

[4] A court of record for the manor held before the lord or his steward.

[5] Alban J., and Thomas, W. S.K., 'Charters of the Borough of Brecon 1276-1517', *Brycheiniog* xxx (1992-3).

[6] Premises at the rear of a dwelling.

Day 6: The Shire Hall, Usk Bridge, Friary, Christ College, County Gaol and Newton; Sir John Games

We will spend most of this, our final day in Brecon, in the suburb of Llanfaes. But first let us take a close look at the Shire Hall in the Bulwark. Following that inspection, we shall view the impressive bridge over the river Usk with its seven arches, and in Llanfaes itself focus our attention on the medieval friary and Christ College, the gaol (now converted into a block of flats, though the governor's house still remains intact), and Newton.

The Shire Hall is, undoubtedly, one of the most imposing buildings in the ancient borough of Brecon, and the visitor approaching the town from the east is immediately impressed. Thomas Roscoe (1791-1871), author and translator, described the building in the early nineteenth century as 'forming a beautiful object to great (sic) the traveller's sight as he enters the town by way of Crickhowell. It stands upon an area, along the side of which extends a public promenade called Captain's Walk, pleasantly shadowed by poplars and sycamores, with the Usk flowing merrily at its base.'

This 'majestic' structure, built of pure Bath stone, was completed in 1842, though there is no record of an official opening ceremony. Its primary purpose was as a venue for the law courts, particularly the Courts of Assize, though public meetings could also be held there. Prior to 1842 the courts, together with meetings of the town council, had been held in the Guild Hall, situated in the High Street. However, the inadequacy of this building, allied to the fact that the partnership between county and town was an unhappy one—they were not ideal bedfellows—resulted in a decision being taken in 1838, at a meeting of the Court of Quarter Sessions, to build forthwith a Shire Hall. A sense of urgency would have been added to proceedings by the fact that, with the demise of the Courts of Great Sessions in 1830, and their replacement by Assize Courts subject to the great courts at Westminster—the union of England and Wales was now complete—Brecon, in 1831, had become an Assize town. A committee was established to inspect possible sites, and it was a garden belonging to a Henry Allen, Esqr., and occupied by Dr Henry Lucas, the father of Thomas Prestwood Lucas, adjoining Captain's Walk, that found universal favour. A presentment was made at a meeting of the Quarter Sessions in January 1839, and in April the choice of site was approved. The land was then purchased for £740, though later, when building was in progress, it was found necessary to purchase other property and additional land to improve the approaches.

Advertisements were now placed in *The Times, The Silurian,* and the *Merthyr Guardian* inviting the submission of designs from architects, in either the Tuscan or Doric styles, and the entry which won final acceptance was that prepared by the firm of Messrs Wyatt and Brandon of Lincoln's Inn Fields, London. The construction work was then put out to tender, and the contract awarded to a local man, Samuel Hancorn.

The successful architect, T. H. Wyatt, was to become one of the leading architects of the Victorian period. He did a considerable amount of work in Breconshire, since he not only designed the Shire Hall, but also prepared plans, in neo-Gothic style, for improving the comfort and seating capacity of the Priory Church. In the south-western extremity of the county, at Craig-y-nos, he was responsible for the blueprint of the house built there by Rhys Powell between 1841-3. It was this house that was purchased in 1878 by the world-famous soprano, Adelina Patti, who spent an estimated £100,000 on enlarging it and extending the estate. Wyatt was enabled to develop his architectural practice in south Wales through family connections, since his uncle, Arthur Wyatt, lived at Troy House, Monmouth, and was agent for the Duke of Beaufort. His other projects in south Wales included the design of the Shire Hall at Monmouth, and the initial restoration of Llandaff Cathedral.

There would appear to have been some delay connected with the negotiations for the land and the raising of the necessary capital, for it was not until April 1841 that a Clerk of Works was appointed at a salary of £2 12*s*. 6*d*. a week. The work now proceeded without any further hitches and an insurance policy of £3,000 was secured. A condition of the policy was that workmen extinguished all candles at the end of the day's work. The iron railings which

The new Shire Hall, 1842.

encompassed the building were erected by a local firm, Hodges and Wright, at a cost of 7*s*. 9*d*. per foot, though the gates cost an additional 10*s*. a foot. The total cost of land and building amounted altogether to £12,000, and the money was raised through loans from local people like Miss Anne Latham of Crickhowell, who contributed £1,800, Mr William Dyke £800, and Mr John Powell, Clerk of the Peace, £5,300. The interest paid on the loans was five per cent, and the capital was to be repaid in equal instalments over a period of ten years.

The completed building contained a spacious courtroom, a large grand-jury room, with a witnesses' waiting room attached, and a judges' robing and retiring room; there was also a counsels' robing room, together with various other offices; furthermore, there was a second courtroom in which Petty Sessions could be held. The first Assize held in the new Shire Hall was conducted before Sir William Henry Maule on 23 March 1843, when there were twenty prisoners for trial, with an additional fifty-four undergoing sentence at the county gaol. The High Sheriff at the time was Walter Maybery.

129

Presiding over the Quarter Sessions and the Assize Court was a judge of the High Court, and he was a barrister of many years standing. He moved around his circuit, travelling from one Assize Court to the next, and when at Brecon his stay would be about eight days.

In the nineteenth century the judge itinerated in a special coach, and, after the advent of the steam engine, in a reserved compartment on a railway coach. These precautions were taken to preclude the possibility of the judge being bribed en route. On arrival at Brecon he would be met by the High Sheriff in formal dress, accompanied by other town dignitaries, who would escort him to his lodgings, County House, in the Struet. The judge always brought his own staff, including a cook, to prevent the possibility of his being poisoned. The ceremonial opening of the Assize Court was always preceded by a service in the Priory Church of St John's which, after 1923, became the Cathedral Church of the new diocese of Swansea and Brecon, and in attendance would be the sheriff, mayor and councillors. Following the service the judge would walk in procession to the Shire Hall. On the first day an armed guard from the camp at Cwrt-y-gollen would be provided; on subsequent days this role would be performed by the local constabulary. Leading the procession would be two trumpeters and, occasionally, a band. Once arrived at the court, the High Sheriff, wearing uniform and carrying a sword, the symbol of royal justice, would accompany the judge to the Bench.

The Quarter Sessions were held every three months and at this court middle-level crimes such as theft, malicious damage, perjury, forgery and sexual offences were tried. Murder and treason cases could not be held there, as the judge lacked the authority to impose the death penalty or life imprisonment. More serious cases were held before the Assize Court. These courts continued to be held in the new Shire Hall until 1971, when they were abolished, and replaced by the Crown Courts sitting at Merthyr Tydfil, so that today there are only magistrates' courts held at Brecon.

Together with being the venue for the courts, the Shire Hall was also a suitable centre for public gatherings of interested people to discuss matters of local importance. In August 1847 a meeting was held there, chaired by the banker, John Parry de Winton, for the purpose of establishing a National School for 150 girls and a similar number of infants in the town. The school was to be erected on a site at the Postern given by a Mr John Powell, and subscriptions for this worthy objective were collected.

Following the abolition of the Quarter Sessions and the Assize Courts, it was decided to adapt the Shire Hall for another use. The museum had hitherto been housed in what was once the Independent chapel in Glamorgan Street, but the edifice was singularly inappropriate for such a purpose. The extinction of the Quarter Sessions and Assize Courts meant that the museum could now be found a more congenial home, and no time was lost in embarking upon the change which entailed considerable structural alterations. Work was commenced in April 1973 and the project completed in January 1974, the total cost amounting to the not inconsiderable sum of £137,829. A focal point of the museum is the courtroom which has been little altered. The principal aim behind the scheme was not the creation of a peaceful haven for scholars, or a secure refuge for those seeking shelter from the elements, but rather the provision of a 'living centre of activity' which people generally would want to visit and enjoy. It was very fitting that the new Brecknock museum should have been officially opened on Thursday, 28 March, 1974 by Canon J. Jones Davies, who had laboured tirelessly for the museum whilst it was in Glamorgan Street, and whose interest in the history and antiquities of Breconshire had been so passionate and enlightened.

Let us now take our leave of the Shire Hall and proceed along Glamorgan Street, past Buckingham Place at the corner, and at the traffic lights we will turn left down Ship Street—an unforgivable corruption of Sheep Street—until we reach the stone bridge over the river Usk. Here let us pause and reflect a little on its history.

Breconshire, because of its numerous rivers and streams, is provided with an abundance of bridges. The most common type, possibly, is the one arch bridge, but the ones that evoke gasps of admiration are those with six, or even seven, arches. At the sight of these the photographer reaches for his camera, and the artist hastily prepares his canvas, brushes and paint.

131

A view of the Usk bridge.

Where the Usk bridge stands today there was, from earliest times, a ford (*rhyd*). Indeed, the Normans called this crossing near their castle Bernard's Ford (*Rhyd Bernard*). But fords are notoriously unreliable for man and beast, since footings can be unstable and, in times of flood, they cannot be used at all. It was inevitable, therefore, that with the passage of time, and increased trafficking along the roads, fords should be replaced by bridges, constructed either of wood or stone, though there is no evidence when the first bridge was built to span the river at *Rhyd Bernard*. However, it was certainly there by the fifteenth century, and so important was it to the inhabitants of Brecon that leading citizens felt obligated to leave legacies in their wills for its repair and maintenance. Roger Gody, a burgess of Brecon, who died in 1407, left 6*s.* 8*d.* for the maintenance of the bridge called 'Redewbrewysbrugge', and it is tempting to surmise that this was the bridge over the Usk. He left a similar amount for a bridge named 'Stonebrugge'. From this it can be deduced, possibly, that the former bridge was built of timber. For two other bridges called 'Laddynbrugge' and 'Hoddenbrugge', the latter being situated on the Honddu near to the fulling mills

(*Pandai*), he donated 3*s.* 4*d.* to each. In the succeeding century, Sir John Price of Priory House (died 1555), the eminent lawyer, civil servant and antiquary, left £10 to be spent at the discretion of the bailiff and his 'two eldest brethren towards the mending of the bridge upon Usk', and the terminology here leaves one in no doubt as to which of the four bridges he intended.

John Leland, the intrepid traveller, who embarked upon an itinerary of England and Wales in the 1530s and 1540s, mentions a bridge over the Usk having been destroyed by heavy floods in 1535, these deluges having been occasioned not by torrential rain but by melting snow from the surrounding mountains. He averred that 'the water ran forward about the top of the high bridge and the circle mark appeareth almost about the middle wall of the Black Friar's Cloister'. Almost thirty years were to elapse before another bridge, certainly of stone, was provided, and it was only in 1563 that the new bridge was completed, as becomes evident from these lines from an old Welsh stanza:

> Nid oedd oedran Iesu lle molant,
> Trugain a three mwy na phum cant,
> Y gnawd peth difethiant,
> Pont ar Wysc mi rho gof i gant.

(It was in the year of our Lord Jesus, who is to be praised, sixty three years beyond 1,500, that an imperishable work was effected; a bridge over the Usk which will provide memories for hundreds).

This was the bridge that so impressed Thomas Churchyard, a poet of Elizabeth's reign (1520?-1604), since he was to pen these lines:

> The river Usk and Honddu runs thereby,
> Four bridges good, of stone stands one each stream,
> The greatest bridge, doth to the college lie.

By the early decades of the seventeenth century the bridge had yet again suffered from the buffetings of the floods and was sadly

133

in need of repair. But while the decayed bridge at Cardiff over the river Taff had provoked protracted, heated, and unseemly public wranglings between town and county as to which was responsible for repairs, no such conflict between public authorities occurred at Brecon. There, responsibility for the repair of the bridge, a vital artery of commerce as far as the borough was concerned, was shared between town and county, the former being responsible for one twenty-fifth part of the total cost of repairs and maintenance.

In 1637 it was adjudged that the £100 rated on the inhabitants and landowners for the immediate repair of the bridge was inadequate, the borough's share of this sum being only £4. Further moneys had to be raised as a matter of urgency before the work could be completed. The surveyors had underestimated the costs involved in the quarrying and carrying of stones, and for digging channels to divert the waters of the river while the work was in progress. Furthermore, a mason, carpenter, and smith had to be employed, and timber and iron purchased. The problems with the maintenance of the bridge, however, stubbornly refused to go away, and repairs to it were to figure in the deliberations of the justices sitting in Quarter Sessions in 1662, 1678, 1680 and 1691 when 40*s.* were expended on the 'great' bridge.

Significantly, the bridge over the Usk was widened in 1794 to accommodate the ever-increasing amount of traffic on the roads. The work was entrusted to Thomas Edwards, a member of the famous bridge-building family of Eglwysilan in Glamorgan. His father, William Edwards (1719-89), was an Independent minister, though he is best remembered as a builder of bridges, or more precisely, the architect of the bridge at Pontypridd, one of the most dangerous and least serviceable of all the large bridges in Wales. Indeed, it was so perilous that, until the middle of the nineteenth century, people preferred to use the nearby ford. However, its unique design, rare beauty, and technical secrets combined to make it the most controversial bridge in Britain and brought its designer lasting fame. The expense involved in widening the bridge at Brecon amounted to £1,000, and in this sum was included the addition of two extra arches at the Llanfaes end to make the gradient to the centre of the bridge easier. This expansion meant that a smithy at the west end of the bridge had to be removed, since it prevented the water from flowing beneath the additional arches. The smith, Richard Bulcot, was, however, awarded a disturbance fee of four guineas. Theophilus Jones, the renowned local antiquary, described the bridge in 1809 as being wide enough to enable two wagons to pass each other with ease. No need, therefore, for any traffic congestion in the future at each end. Edwards had undertaken to maintain the bridge for seven years so that when, in 1801, the bridge had to be repaired again, his widow protested, not without reason, that the stipulated period had expired. She finally agreed to pay £150, a very shrewd move, as at the next meeting of the Quarter Sessions the justices awarded the contract to John Maund of Tŷ Mawr in the parish of Llanelli who undertook to repair the bridge for £423. He further agreed to maintain it for twenty-one years for an annual payment of five guineas.

In 1803, shortly after the bridge was repaired, the river immediately above the bridge, on the Watergate and Kensington side, bore witness to an historic event. A mass public baptism took place there, probably the first occasion on which such a service had occurred in the town, though something similar could possibly have happened during the Commonwealth Period (1649-1660). The officiating minister was the Rev. David Evans of Dolau, and the novelty of the occasion attracted a large concourse of people on a lovely Sabbath morning, curious to witness proceedings. Many of the onlookers watching from the bridge, and from the bank on the opposite side of the river, had come to scoff though, in the event, many remained to pray. During the ritual of baptism, which was conducted to a background of jeering, a water bird which had been flying over people's heads, and skimming low over the water, suddenly alighted on the head of the minister. The tumult immediately subsided, and the final acts of baptism were conducted in complete silence, and in an atmosphere of some solemnity.

The Usk bridge formed a kind of umbilical cord linking the town with developments beyond the river. In the Middle Ages Brecon had gradually outgrown its walls, and suburbs had developed in extra-mural areas like Llanfaes in the west, the Watton in the east, and the Struet in the north. In Llanfaes much of the lord's demesne land had been located. Here were to be found his meadows and his pastures, and on these lands he had grazed his sheep and his cattle, his swine and his geese. Even his stallion or war horse had been stabled there, cared for by his bondmen as part of their customary service.

The spiritual needs of this suburban population came to be provided for by the Black Friars, who built a house near the highway and, a few hundred yards further along the road, the little chapel of St David, consisting of a chancel, nave and tower. Giraldus Cambrensis, who found it difficult to resist recounting stories of a miraculous nature, relates the tale of the boy whose hand, whilst he was in the act of removing some young pigeons from their nest within the church, stuck to the stone on which he was leaning. It took three days of prayer and supplication before it was finally released. While spiritual nourishment would have been provided by these two religious institutions, the physical needs of the inhabitants were partly met by the salmon and trout to be found in abundance in the Usk, Tarell, and Honddu. And their activities as fishermen were not confined to local streams and rivers, because it is known that widows and unmarried daughters trekked as far as Llangorse Lake to cast their nets into its waters.

Llanfaes was one of the twelve wards of Brecon,[1] and law and order were enforced by two constables appointed at the Court Leet. Judging from the Rent Roll of 1664, the district appears to have had a most pleasant aspect, since it was given over almost entirely to houses and gardens, though the tuckers appear to have dwelt there in significant numbers. It was the smallest of the wards, and as the land was low-lying, and bounded by two rivers, the Usk and the Tarell, it was subject to frequent flooding, much to the justifiable annoyance and dismay of the inhabitants. This problem was not to be overcome until 1983 when proper flood defences were built. By the early nineteenth century the character of Llanfaes had changed considerably. There was a great deal of poor housing, and it had the unenviable reputation of being the worst district in the town. On Saturday nights such were the drunkenness and violence that it was virtually a 'no-go' area for law-abiding citizens. Even the police did not venture to enter there singly.

Gambling was rife, particularly in inns like the 'Flag and Castle'. One inhabitant, who wished for obvious reasons to remain anonymous, wrote in 1842 to the bailiff complaining of these iniquities which, to him, had assumed such proportions 'that a decent female cannot pass the streets in safety'. Doubtless his view was slightly jaundiced because at that time Brecon was seething with religious activity, exemplified, amongst other things, by a rash of chapel building. However, the substance of his allegations could well have been true.

The site on which Christ College now stands is undoubtedly the most interesting in Llanfaes, as it has been in continuous occupation for at least seven hundred years. Over the centuries three different institutions have stood there, all closely related to the church. The earliest foundation (*c.* 1250), was the Dominican Friary of St Nicholas, the patron saint of children; the second (1541), was a sixteenth-century endowed grammar school, and the third (1853) a modern public school.

The Dominican Friars built their church, together with its conventual buildings, on this site *c.* 1250. A single or possibly a double cloister connected the church to the present dining halls.

Brecon Friary: the dining halls.

137

The style of architecture of the church was predominantly Early English, though there is some Decorated work. Such was the elegance of the structure that Welsh bards were inspired to indulge in wild encomiums and flights of poetic fancy, and extravagant comparisons were drawn between it and the Church of Rome and Jerusalem. According to Lewis Glyn Cothi or Llywelyn y Glyn (1447-86), one of the greatest of the fifteenth-century Welsh poets, and a devoted supporter of Jasper Tudor, Henry Tudor's uncle, the local gentry, including the Games family just down the road at Newton, and the Awbreys of Abercynrig, were content to find a final resting place with the Black Friars. The house flourished until the fourteenth century, when a north aisle and a chapel were added. The smaller of the dining halls was also built in this century. Despite its location in the suburbs of a town, it is quite possible that many of the brothers were recruited from among the local Welsh, and that they played a leading part in bringing religion to their fellow countrymen in their own tongue. From the latter half of the fourteenth century, decline set in amongst the mendicants generally. There are indications of a lowered vitality, and their influence was on the wane. When the friars were finally swept away by parliamentary *diktat* in 1538 few voices were raised in protest and lamentation.

However, the friary at Brecon, as well as being a final resting place for the local gentry, attracted the living also, and pilgrims flocked there to venerate the rood, or great cross, of the church, which enjoyed a considerable vogue as a source of miraculous cures. The friary would have profited from their offerings, just as it benefited from the bequests of the wealthy. The earliest known benefactor was Eleanor of Castile, Edward I's Queen, who, in 1271, left a small legacy to the house. Another donor was Humphrey de Bohun (IX), a powerful magnate and the lord of Brecon, who left £10 to the friars to pray for him. This stream of charitable bequests continued to be made to the friary right up to the time of its dissolution.

Despite these legacies, forces were unleashed on Welsh society in the fourteenth and fifteenth centuries, such as the Black Death and the revolt of Owain Glyndŵr, which exercised a debilitating effect on religious houses, so that at the end of the Middle Ages they presented a spectacle of decay. When Henry VIII and his chief minister, Thomas Cromwell, embarked upon the destruction of the friaries, they were already in a deplorably reduced condition with their depleted communities deeply in debt and low in morale.

The visitation of the Welsh friaries to establish the state of the morals of the brothers, and the quality of their religious life, was entrusted by Cromwell to Richard Ingworth, bishop of Dover, and himself a former friar. He opened his inspection of the friaries in south Wales from Brecon. The procedure adopted for the suppression of a friary was straightforward enough. On arrival at a friary he would summon the inmates by ringing the convent bell. Once assembled, he would proceed to inform them that he only desired to effect reforms. Certain portions of their rule would then be read out, and he would enquire whether they were able to conduct themselves in accordance with them. If they were unable to do so, he would accept their surrender. The deed of surrender of the house at Brecon ran as follows: 'We, the prior of the Convent of the Black Friars of Brecknock with one assent and consent, without any coercion or counsel, do give our house into the hands of the lord visitor to the King's use desiring his Grace to be good and gracious to us. In witness we subscribe our names with our proper hands the XXIX day of August, in the XXXth year of the reign of our most dread Sovereign lord King Henry the VIIIth'. Two, at least, of the friars were illiterate and made their mark only. It was in this manner that the Black Friars disappeared forever from the Brecon scene. No longer would they be seen preaching at street corners; no longer would they be heard singing in their little chapel. One cannot but bewail their fate, for the last prior, Richard David, and his nine friars, unlike the abbots and monks, were thrust out into an uncaring world without grants or pensions to keep body and soul together, though Bishop Barlow of St David's had promised that he would provide honest livings for the friars of Brecon. It can only be hoped that he kept his word. The possessions of the friary at its dissolution in 1538 were very meagre. There were no chalices or jewels; its possessions simply consisted of a few gardens, orchards, tenements and meadows to the annual value of £3 5*s.* It could be that Richard David had anticipated the axe falling, for prior to the destruction of the house some of the meadows belonging to it had been leased out to local laymen and particularly to one Llywelyn ap Morgan.

Parts of the friary were now reduced to rubble as the lead, dressed stone and seasoned timber were removed by the local gentry and townspeople to be used for their own particular purposes. Today, all that remains of the Dominican Friary is the chapel and both dining halls; and they represent the largest group of Dominican buildings surviving in Britain. However, the site was not to lie waste for long. Three years later, in 1541, the same King whose powerful will had wreaked such havoc in the 1530s, established an institution there for the promotion of learning. This foundation came to be known as the College of Christ or Christ College and was the first of its kind in Wales.

Bishop Richard Rawlins of St David's had been the first to urge the translation of the College of prebends from Abergwili, outside Carmarthen, to Brecon, and he had portrayed the inhabitants of the 'principal town of South Wales' as being illiterate and beggarly 'ignorant alike of their duty to God and man'. His plea fell on deaf ears, but when his successor at the diocese, William Barlow, a zealous Protestant, renewed it with further scathing remarks about the 'barefoot rascals of Brecon', Henry finally paid heed and consented to the move despite the emotional opposition of the people of Abergwili.

The teaching staff of the new foundation consisted of a master, an usher, a lecturer in divinity, and a stipendiary priest; the grammar master receiving £13 6*s.* 8*d.* annually, while the usher, lecturer and priest each got £6 13*s.* 4*d.* In the event, the master, James Faber, received £20 since he combined his office with that of lecturer. Free education was offered to all who wished to receive it, and an annual sum of £24 was set aside for the maintenance of first twenty, and later, twenty-four poor scholars. The revenue to sustain the college was derived from two principal sources: first, and by far the most lucrative, was the income from the prebends. There were twenty-two prebendaries, each of whom was expected to make a donation from his clerical income towards the upkeep of the school. From the Chantry Certificate of 1548, sixteen are listed as having contributed a total of £26 13*s.* 5*d.* between them; secondly, the lands which had belonged to the friary had now been transferred to the college, and the revenue raised by leasing these meadows to laymen was another source of income, though rather meagre to say the least.

Christ College.

A school day of eight hours duration was very demanding for the scholars. The boys, whose ages could vary from eight to twenty, were taught together in the one room, and discipline was extremely severe. Learning was by rote, and within the curriculum the emphasis was on the teaching of Latin grammar and literature, together with a little Greek, and some provision was made for religious education. There was no room for the teaching of mathematics, the sciences, or foreign languages and, unlike the situation today, there were few opportunities for playing games. English was the medium of instruction, and the use of Welsh was actively discouraged. The basic purpose behind the establishment of Christ College was undoubtedly political; it was to inculcate the virtue of obedience to state and church, to King, bishop and magistrate. In other words the powers that be expected the school to mould its pupils into good citizens. The emphasis on Latin arose to some extent from a vocational need, as it was inconceivable that anyone should enter any ecclesiastical, diplomatic, or legal post without a knowledge of it. The ability to decline *mensa* opened the doors to the world of work and opportunity.

But the good intentions of the royal founder were never to be fully realised. When Archbishop George Abbot made his visitation of the diocese of St David's in 1614, he found the college chapel at Brecon in a state of decay, its services discontinued, and the payments due to the teaching staff in arrears. This situation had largely arisen because of the negligence of the prebendaries who had ignored the stipulation in the foundation charter that they should reside there.

Many illustrious bishops became connected with the college. A much celebrated one was William Laud who, when Bishop of St David's (1621-6), undertook several visitations of his extensive see. The first of these took place on 9 July 1622, when he preached at the college. Later, Laud became Archbishop of Canterbury (1633), and he stirred up a hornet's nest by his policy of High Anglicanism within the church and, in the realm of politics, preaching the divine right of Kings and upholding their prerogative powers. Such was his unpopularity that, in 1645, in a mean spirit of revenge, the victorious parliamentarians led this brave old man—he was seventy-two years of age—to the scaffold. Another bishop of St David's who took a keen interest in the college was the Hampshire man, Dr William Lucy. Another High Churchman, to the Anglicans he was a shining star; among the Dissenters, however, like Laud, he is remembered as a vengeful persecutor. A less controversial and more popular bishop was the saintly George Bull who became bishop of St David's in 1705. He was a theologian with a European reputation, and he contributed much to restoring the tarnished image of Christ College following the maladministration of his predecessor, Thomas Watson, whose misconduct led to his suspension, trial and deprivation. At Christ College, throughout the centuries, a pattern of reform and restoration, followed by neglect and decay, has been repeated. One moment the college has ridden high on the crest of a wave; the next moment it has been found at the bottom of a deep trough.

But Christ College has also produced luminaries amongst its headteachers and pupils. An outstanding headteacher in the eighteenth century, and, incidentally, the longest serving one to date (1757-1801), was David Griffiths who did much to promote a greatly needed renaissance in the school's fortunes during a century when the college, for the most part, was stagnating. Under his enlightened leadership Christ College nurtured the talents of a number of outstanding pupils. Amongst the students who were to achieve considerable distinction in various walks of national life are to be found Theophilus Jones, the eminent historian of Brecknockshire, who later warmly described David Griffiths as 'the respected and respectable preceptor of my youth'; the Rev. Edward Davies, author of *Horae Britannicae*; Dr Thomas Coke, the father of American Methodism; Thomas Price (Carnhuanawc), one of the leading Celtic scholars of his day; and Dr John Jones, the litigious theologian and scholar.

However, the eighteenth century, despite the peaks as exemplified by the headmastership of David Griffiths, was a period when the college was in a state of decadence. The bishops of St David's who succeeded Lucy and Bull were greedy and apathetic in their attitude towards the college, and many of the prebendaries had ceased to contribute towards its upkeep. Its lamentable state was revealed in the Charity Commissioners' Report of 1836, by which time the number of pupils had been reduced to seven. Important contributory factors in this decline were the narrowness of the curriculum, and the opening, in 1825, of St David's College, Lampeter. By 1840 the chapel had lost much of its roof, and neighbouring farmers were using the building as a stable on market days. As for the school, it had been forced to migrate to rooms in the town itself, in Lion Street and Bell Lane. In 1845 the school closed, and it remained closed for two years.

Christ College, in possibly the darkest hour in its history, was to be saved by the intervention of powerful public figures. In 1846 the

Rev. Jermyn Pratt who, though living in Norfolk, had close connections with Brecon, since he was related to Lord Camden, a substantial landowner in the district, now took up the cudgels on behalf of the college; and Lord Camden himself was not indifferent, for he had written to Colonel Thomas Wood, the M.P. for Breconshire, who also added his considerable weight. The Rev. Hugh Bold, another well-connected cleric, declared in a letter to the Church Commissioners that he could not 'reconcile himself to the idea of allowing so ancient, and so well-endowed an establishment to fall to ruin'. Sir Benjamin Hall, later created Lord Llanover, now rushed pell-mell into the fray, and vigorously supported Pratt against Bishop Connop Thirwall of St David's, who had criticised Pratt for his 'very partial and inaccurate statement'. Neither did the bishop spare Hall, whom he accused of 'voluntary ignorance' and of 'flinging accusations at a venture'. To strengthen and verify his case Hall now dispatched his agent, William Llewellin, to Brecon to compile a report on the state of the college. Pratt's findings, made five years earlier, were corroborated by him.

The restoration of the college and its buildings had now become a matter of grave necessity, particularly as the Nonconformists were making such headway in Brecon. Llewellin estimated that there were seven chapels within eight hundred yards of Christ College, at four of which the services were conducted in Welsh, whereas the Established Church offered only one Welsh service a fortnight at St David's. The Anglicans were further embarrassed by the fact that the Catholics, reinvigorated by the lifting of legal restrictions on their activities, had just completed the building of a new church, in the Gothic style, in St Michael's Street.

Another champion now entered the lists. This was the Rev. Basil Jones, and he, too, presented convincing arguments to protect the college's future. Sympathisers with the college now found it essential to enter powerful pleadings on its behalf, for there were clamorous voices raised opposed to its re-establishment. It was argued by the college's opponents that any new endowments should be bestowed on the college at Lampeter or the more recently established college at Llandovery. The debate resulted in a scheme being prepared in the Court of Chancery in 1851, and the Christ

College Act of Parliament, embodying its proposals, became law in 1853. It was by the terms of this act that a modern public school, with the Rev. J. D. Williams, at the tender age of twenty-six, the first headmaster, and provided with its own board of governors, came into being in 1855.

The re-founding of the school was followed by an intensive building programme. Apart from the dilapidation, prior to 1853 the use of buildings at Christ College had been totally inappropriate. The earliest accurate plan of the buildings in 1851 shows the schoolroom to have been adjacent to a slaughterhouse. In close proximity also were the pigsties, a dunghill, and a tannery. Even allowing for the fact that susceptibilities then were not as delicate as they are today, this environment was hardly conducive to the promotion of sound learning. Between 1860-90 the Victorian buildings, which so nicely complement the medieval survivals, made their appearance. These included a headmaster's residence, dormitories, the library, and Donaldson House. Furthermore, the chapel, which had been reduced to such a sorry state, was sympathetically restored by Sir Gilbert Scott who, at the time, was also busily involved with the renovation of the priory church. These developments made possible a rapid increase in the number of pupils and, to accommodate the demands of mid-Victorian society, a hitherto predominantly classical curriculum was expanded to embrace English grammar, writing, geography, history, arithmetic, mathematics, and such other languages and branches of literature, art and science as the governors should prescribe. Games such as cricket, soccer, and rugby also now became an integral part of school life.

In the twentieth century the school continued to expand—there were additions to the playing fields as well as the accommodation —and it had to adapt still further to meet the challenges of a rapidly changing world. Science came to occupy a far more important role in the curriculum, and chemistry and physics laboratories were built. A recognition of the prominence given to science is seen in the appointment of a new breed of headmaster. Until 1962 they were, without exception, in the classical mould; since the appointment of Dr J. Sharp in that year, they have all been scientists. These changes were also accompanied by a radical reorganisation of teaching space. In the two World Wars, 1914-18, and 1939-45, boys from the school fought and fell, and many were decorated for conspicuous gallantry. In 1985 there occurred a change of momentous importance, and one which reflected the altered status of women in society. For the first time in its 450-year history, girls were admitted, and a bastion of male chauvinism had finally fallen. It can now only be a matter of time before a headmistress replaces a headmaster. As a result of this revolutionary development, new games like girls' hockey and netball have appeared on the fixture list. The whole ethos of the school has been changed, and doubtless for the better. But Christ College is accustomed to change. Chameleon-like, over the centuries, it has been forced to adapt, and it is this ability to respond to altering circumstances that has contributed to making the college one of the foremost independent schools in Wales today.

Having partially absorbed the atmosphere of an ancient friary and a modern public school, let us now travel westwards through Llanfaes along the A40. At the far end of the suburb, near the Tarell bridge, on the left hand side of the road, there is located the prison governor's house which had been built immediately outside the gaol walls. Between 1974-76, the gaol was converted into a block of flats so that today it is very difficult to envisage a prison, where debtors and felons were incarcerated, having existed there at all. It is even more difficult to imagine public hangings taking place outside its sturdy walls.

The common gaol had once been situated in the castle, but following the slighting of the castle during the Civil War, wrongdoers were detained in a prison situated near the Struet gate. It remained in the possession of the corporation until 1842, though it was rarely used as a place of confinement after 1800. This was hardly surprising since in 1779, according to John Howard, the famous philanthropist and prison reformer, it simply consisted of two small rooms. There were no fireplaces, no courts, no water, and the house was in a dilapidated condition. But the main reason for its abandonment is to be found in the fact that in 1690 a new

Brecon gaol in 1969. (courtesy of Brecknock Museum)

county gaol had been erected in the Watton, on a site currently occupied by the Trustees Savings Bank. When Howard inspected this gaol in 1774 he found it, in turn, to be in a sad state of repair, with debtors and felons huddled indiscriminately together in two courts. The prisoners were not even provided with the luxury of a little straw on which to lie. The gaoler was paid an annual salary of £31 10*s.* and from this sum he was expected to feed the prisoners. It can readily be surmised that the fare provided would barely have been sufficient to keep body and soul together.

In 1781 a new gaol and House of Correction, designed to hold twenty-four prisoners, was erected on the east bank of the Tarell in the parish of St David's. The builder, Andrew Maund, was a local man, and he was also the owner of the Theatre Royal in the Watton. In one court of the new bridewell the accommodation consisted of five day rooms for debtors, a day room for male felons with two cells attached, and a lodging room; in another court there were five more cells. The women were confined in a separate court provided with a day room, five lodging rooms, together with two rooms for the sick. There was also a chapel. Howard visited this gaol shortly after it was built (1782), and he was singularly unimpressed by it. It

147

was not particularly clean, and was subject to flooding. Indeed, shortly before his arrival, it had been flooded to a depth of three feet. There were times when security at the gaol left much to be desired. Many attempts at escape had been made, and some had been successful. Furthermore, discipline could be lax, and one governor, John Rice, had been accused of 'culpable negligence'. This prison was also cold, nor would an ill-balanced diet of gruel, potatoes, and bread have enabled the prisoners to build up a great deal of body heat. When a number of justices inspected it in 1841, it appeared to them that the method of warming certain areas was 'cruelly insufficient, and particularly during inclement weather'. Another problem was overcrowding, and in the 1840s, to relieve pressure on space, an application was made to the Home Secretary for permission to transfer some prisoners to gaols in neighbouring counties.

The need for more space led to consideration being given to enlarging the gaol, though the increase in the county rate which would inevitably have followed meant that little was done until 1858, when an additional male wing was added at a cost of £5,000. It contained forty cells, each of which was capable of holding three persons. In 1870 what remained of the old 'Newgate' was razed to the ground, and a replacement block built at a cost of £8,000. At the same time, adjacent to the gaol, a prison governor's house was built. The whole project represented a considerable rebuilding programme, and the substantial amount of money required to construct a more modern, secure, and greatly expanded gaol, was raised from the Crown Insurance Company, which charged an interest rate of 4½ per cent. It was further agreed that the loan should be repaid in thirty equal instalments. While work on the new gaol was in progress, another 'home' had to be found for the prisoners, and it was for this reason that they were transferred to the gaol in Hereford at a cost of 10s. a head per week.

Official visitors to the gaol liked what they saw. Tribute was paid to 'the excellence of its internal arrangements', and to the 'able and humane management'. Furthermore, no complaints were received from the prisoners, and the building throughout was extremely clean. In 1878 the administration of the prison was transferred into the hands of the Secretary of State, thus effectively ending local control. This year also witnessed the retirement of the longest serving of the prison governors, John Lazenby. A London policeman, Lazenby had been first introduced to Wales when, as one of a contingent of 'bobbies', he had been dispatched to Carmarthenshire to help quell the disturbances there. He was appointed to the office of governor in 1837, and held it for a period of forty-one years. His wife, too, had been involved with the administration of the prison, as she had held the post of matron. Both were awarded pensions, richly deserved one would have thought, his being £165 a year while hers was substantially less at £57.

During John Lazenby's tenure of office there had been three public hangings in Brecon. In each case the crime had been murder and the motive greed, and at the northern end of the prison yard three simple headstones had marked the malefactors' final resting places. The names of these murderers were Thomas Thomas, James Griffiths alias Tom Williams, and William Williams, and the crimes had taken place at Trecastle, Cwmgwdi, and Crickhowell respectively.

Thomas Thomas had killed a Cardiganshire farmer by the name of David Lewis. The victim, accompanied by his son aged twelve, had taken two carts of butter and other provisions to the 'works' somewhere in the industrial valleys of south Wales, and was returning home via Brecon and Trecastle. At Brecon, he had been engaged in conversation by Thomas, and Lewis, probably slightly inebriated, had let slip that he was carrying on his person a substantial amount of money. Thomas now accompanied Lewis on his way home, and the little boy having gone ahead with one cart, both men got out of the other about a mile from Trecastle. Thomas then drew a pistol and shot Lewis dead. He proceeded to rob the dead man before returning hurriedly to his home in Carmarthenshire. On the following day he was arrested and, after due trial at the Assizes in Brecon, on Thursday, 10 April 1845, he was publicly hanged, and his execution, it would appear, was witnessed by some 15,000 people. Most would have been attracted through sheer curiosity; others because they craved a cheap thrill. But doubtless there were some present, and this is a sobering thought, simply

149

because they were sadistic and vengeful, and relished the taking of another person's life. The church bells would have been rung, and at night, in the many inns of Brecon, huge quantities of beer would have been quaffed, and the town would have presented a spectacle of riotous drunkenness.

Four years later another murder most foul was committed at Cwmgwdi at the foot of the Brecon Beacons. The murderer was an extremely handsome youth of eighteen who, for a little financial gain, killed a fellow farm worker by the name of Thomas Griffiths in the chaff-room of the farm. He had bided his opportunity, and when Griffiths had bent over during the course of his work, he had struck him repeatedly with an axe. He had then attempted to hide the body in a dunghill, but had been disturbed by the arrival of a servant girl. Throwing away the fork which he had been using, he had entered the house and taken possession of the dead man's clothes, together with one gold sovereign and eight shillings in silver, before departing for Merthyr where he hoped to lose himself amongst the toiling masses there. After a week in Merthyr, on hearing a report of the murder, he made his way first to Swansea and then Bristol. He was now a fugitive, and the authorities, together with Colonel Lloyd Vaughan Watkins of Penoyre, M.P., had posted rewards for his apprehension. He now roved around the south of England before being finally arrested at Stowmarket for stealing a cake and placed in Ipswich gaol. He was returned to Brecon, and stood trial for his heinous crime at the Spring Assizes of 1849. Sentenced to death, he was hanged at Brecon gaol before a crowd estimated at between 12,000 to 15,000 people, probably a gross exaggeration. The onlookers were quiet and restrained during the execution, but in the evening the drunkenness 'defied all description'.

Brecon was to witness its last public execution in 1861. The murderer, again, was a young man of only nineteen. His name was William Williams, and he had killed his aunt at Grwyne-fawr, near Crickhowell, on 19 October 1860. The following March he was sentenced to death at the Brecon Assizes and, on the morning of 23 April 1861, he breathed his last on the gallows before 3,000 to 4,000 people. His object had been to gain possession of the little homestead to which he considered himself the heir. It was for this reason that he had reached for the gun over the mantelpiece and, in cold blood, shot his aunt dead. During the trial he had endeavoured, in his own defence, to implicate others, but before the trapdoor was sprung he had made a full confession. 'I feel I am prepared to die. I have had six months to prepare to die, but my poor aunt had not a moment to do so. I die justly'.

A public hanging did not come cheaply. At the Brecon Sessions held in April 1817, David Edwards, a young man of twenty-three years of age, was sentenced to death for 'wilfully, maliciously and unlawfully cutting Gwenllian Morgan, spinster, with intent to murder her'. Charles Claude Clifton, who was sheriff of the county at the time, and in that capacity responsible for ensuring that the execution was carried out according to law, had paid the expenses incurred out of his own pocket. Following the execution, which had taken place on 9 May 1817, he had applied to the Lords of the Treasury for reimbursement. The total amount claimed had amounted to £22 8s. 10d. The disbursements were made up as follows: the executioner, £5 5s.; a frock for the executioner, 12s.; erecting the gallows, £4 8s. 4d.; the use of a cart to convey the prisoner to the gallows, £1; twelve javelin men, £6 6s.; thirty special constables, £3 17s. 6d.; for tolling the bells at four different churches, £1.

So we bid farewell to the place where once debtors, thieves, and murderers paid their final debt to society, and move across the Tarell bridge. Beyond the bridge, on the right, set a hundred yards or so back from the road, and surrounded by a nine-hole golf course, is located Newton House, one of the ancestral homes of the Games family.

The founder of the family, and its most illustrious member, was Dafydd Gam who, in Welsh history, has acquired a semi-legendary status. Outlawed for cutting down a relative, Richard Fawr of Slwch, in the High Street of Brecon, he had fled to the court of the English king, Henry IV, to whom he was known, since Henry was lord of Brecon. Dafydd was implacably opposed to Owain Glyndŵr, and was even captured by the Welsh rebel chieftain, from whose clutches he was only released following the payment of a considerable ransom. A loyal Lancastrian, he fought for Henry V against the French at Agincourt in 1415 and was slain. According to tradition, a grateful monarch knighted Dafydd on the field of battle before he died of his wounds. His family became considerable landowners in Breconshire, and from their great houses at Newton, Aberbrân, Tregaer, Buckland and Penderyn they played an important role in the county's affairs as sheriffs, recorders, justices of the peace, bailiffs, mayors and parliamentary represent-atives. Sadly, in 1657, the male line died out with Hoo Games.

The Gameses as an important local gentry family, and to demonstrate their wealth and position of superiority, built a new and most impressive house for themselves on the foundations of an earlier dwelling at Newton. The builder was John Games (d. 1613) who was three times sheriff of Breconshire—1574, 1587 and 1596—and he erected this family seat in Llanfaes in substantially its present form in 1582. Much of the building material was obtained from the dissolved friary of St Nicholas which was conveniently near, and where there was to be found a veritable quarry of dressed stone.[2] Newton is extremely important architecturally as it is the earliest example in Wales of the double-pile plan. The medieval hall had normally been only one room wide, and this single room would have occupied the full height of the building. It was heated by an open hearth in the centre of the floor, and the smoke would have escaped through a hole in the roof. Additional space was provided by endways extension, a plan that made for great elongation and awkward circulation. It was in this manner that a two- or three-unit house came into being. The three-unit house would have consisted of a hall, a cross passageway, and below the entrance passage a service room, and beyond the hall a retiring room. The walls were made of stone, or were timber-framed with the panels filled with wattle and daub. A cruck-truss would have supported the roof, which would have been made of stone, slate, or thatch. Windows were usually unglazed, and consisted of closely spaced wooden mullions. To keep out draughts and rain, shutters would have been provided. During the great rebuilding which took place in parts of Wales between 1550-1640,

Newton from the north.

a significant change took place in house construction. Houses of two storeys became general, and permanent staircases, chimneys and fireplaces made their appearance. Initially, all that happened was that the hall was floored over and a stair and fireplace added. Gradually, however, the cruck-truss was supplanted by the box-frame structure. Naturally, these houses would have varied markedly in the details of their construction, particularly with regard to the point of entry and the siting of the fireplace. In north Wales houses with an inside cross passage and chimneys on the outside end walls were common, whereas in south Wales the usual point of entry was at the end of the house. The new houses of mid Wales were different in that the chimney was to be found mostly in the centre.

The double-pile plan or box-frame had positive advantages as it provided for much better circulation, and was much easier to warm, since each room had less external wall. Newton is nearly square. At the rear there are three main storeys, but only two at the front to allow for the hall. The ground floor at the rear is occupied by a parlour, kitchen and stairway.

At Newton, the Gameses, in conformity with the accepted conventions of sixteenth-century society, patronised a family bard (*bardd teulu*). In return for hospitality and gifts, his role was to educate the children and to indulge in fulsome flattery of his patron's virtues. An early bard associated with the Gameses of Newton was born in Merioneth. His name was Huw Cae Llwyd, and he settled in Brecon in 1456. It was he who lamented, in exaggerated style, the passing of his benefactor, Morgan ap Dafydd Gam:

> Llai yw hindda yn Llanddwy
> Ac i Lanfaes y Glaw'n fwy

(There is less fine weather in Llanddew, and for Llanfaes there is more rain).

Following Huw's departure for Rome in 1475, he was replaced at Newton by his son, Ieuan ap Huw Cae Llwyd (c. 1475-1560), who had probably been born in Brecon. The beauty of the town was such that he was inspired to pen these lines:

> Llys a gynnal pob eilfyw
> Llanfaes gorau lle i fyw

(A court which sustains every other, Llanfaes is the best place in which to live).

Edward Games, the father of John Games the builder of Newton, and Brecon's parliamentary representative and first recorder, had exaggerated encomiums lavished upon him, though posthumously, by William Llŷn. Acknowledged as a *pencerdd* (chief of song) in the Caerwys Eisteddfod of 1567 at the early age of thirty-three, the poet had travelled extensively all over Wales, and one of his ports of call was Brecon where he enjoyed the hospitality of the Games family:

> Glan Hodni, gwae di fel gwayw dart ydoedd
> Wedi dwyn y llewfart,
> Lle bu'r haul pur ymhob part
> Niwl ydwyd yn ol Eduart.

(Bank of the Honddu, woe to thee like a painful arrow was the death of the leopard. Where the bright sun shone in every part, mist thou art after Edward's death).

John Games, Edward's son, shared with the other gentry of Wales a tremendous pride in pedigree—*llinach*—and his descent from Dafydd Gam becomes clearly evident, and is given considerable prominence, in the inscription over the fireplace in the great hall at Newton.[3]

The hall fireplace with its inscription. (courtesy of Brecknock Museum)

155

He was possessed, like Sir John Wynn of Gwydir, of a violently passionate temperament, and his fractiousness resulted in his getting involved in assaults, affrays, and other misdemeanours such as suborning juries. Some of these disturbances even involved members of his own family, though such family feuds were only too typical of the Welsh social scene at the time. He was described by William Howell, the bailiff of Brecon in 1591, as a 'gentleman of great countenance in the county, well kinned and allied . . . altogether disposed to quarrel and brawl and presuming in respect of his greatness that none . . . durst offer to punish correct or imprison any of his followers'. These retainers were only too often involved in attacks on property and assaults on individuals, and the victims of these outrages claimed that they represented a form of intimidation to enable John Games to have his own way. John Games, however, viewed himself in an entirely different light. In 1591, while residing at Lambeth in Surrey, he described himself as 'inclined to quietness . . . to live peaceably and quietly and to procure his servants and friends to do the like'. He even went so far as to complain of disturbances in Breconshire, including an assault on his home at Newton by more than twenty associates of John Games of Aberbrân, who threatened his wife with a dagger, and called her an 'arrant whore'. It could be, indeed, that this was a classic example of the pot calling the kettle black.

In the 1590s John Games became involved in a long running vendetta with the corporation of Brecon culminating in a series of hotly contested Star Chamber cases. Such was the heat engendered by the dispute that acts of naked aggression were committed in the streets of the ancient borough and honest citizens remained indoors. In 1589, in a case involving Sir David Williams of Gwernyfed, the town's recorder, John Games, who was sheriff of the county at the time, had been openly contemptuous of the authority of the bailiff, and further displayed an utter lack of respect for one of the Queen's officials. In his deposition to Star Chamber David Williams had declared that he had been assaulted in broad daylight by John Games and his followers on the occasion of the holding of the town's Quarter Sessions in the Guild Hall. They had fully intended to murder him, and he was only saved by the intervention of his friends and servants, two of whom had received wounds to their heads. David Williams had been forced to take refuge in Priory House,[4] the home of Gregory Price. On the following day there was more rioting, and David Williams was compelled to abandon the court and return home. An interesting feature of this affair is that the principal players were gentlemen who knew each other well. After all, David Williams's first wife was the daughter of the Games of Aberbrân. It is also very difficult to avoid coming to the conclusion that John Games was endeavouring to prevent a case in which he, in one way or another was involved, from coming to court.

This incident represented the second occasion in 1589 when, despite the prohibition against the carrying of arms on such occasions as the holding of law courts, weapons had been openly displayed during the sessions, and it brought a sharp reprimand from the Privy Council. In a letter to the Brecknock justices they were instructed to 'use all good necessary means for the reformation of these disorders, in the total suppressing in the carrying of weapons in times of sessions and such like assemblies . . . if you should find any disobedient to such orders, then to certify us of their names . . . that we may take such order therein as shall be requisite'.

Two years later, in 1591, John Games again challenged the authority of the town's bailiff. Trouble flared when the bailiff, William Howell, punished Games's friends and kinsmen for selling wines at excessive prices. John Games retaliated by arranging for his servants to present charges against the bailiff on the grounds of his sundry malpractices hoping in that way to destroy his reputation. The charges sounded convincing enough. The bailiff, 'a man of haughty stomach and contentious humour,' had allegedly assembled a number of armed rioters and attacked the house of William Meredith Games, 'a quiet gentleman', for three hours, threatening to summon the town's inhabitants to his assistance by ringing the common Bell.[5] William Meredith Games had finally been apprehended and incarcerated in the common gaol for three days 'without cause'. On another occasion the bailiff had arrested a man without a warrant. A third charge arose from the fact that the bailiff, 'a greedy man', and a mercer 'desiring to impoverish other mercers', had driven those mercers who were not freemen of the borough, out of the town. In his defence William Howell had declared that William Meredith Games was harbouring a man wanted to appear before the Council in Wales and the Marches and he had been instructed to detain him. To that intent he had summoned an alderman, a serjeant-at-mace, and other burgesses to accompany him. The fugitive had managed to make good his escape, but Games was also keeping an unlicensed tavern, and was permitting unlawful games to be played at his house 'in the upper end of Sheep Street'.

The wanted man had been involved in 'outrages committed in the church of Christ College in Brecon' by the servants of John Games. According to William Howell the court action was intended 'to cloak and shadow the sundry and heinous misdemeanours of his suitors and retainers of John Games' and to frighten the town authorities 'from attempting to chastise and reform the bad and lewd conversation, riots and outrages' of John Games's retainers. Howell refuted the charge that he was using his high office to promote his business interests, though he did not deny driving the traders out of town.

In 1592 the two families of Awbrey and Games were at each other's throats, a continuation of a long-standing feud. Trouble which had started in the fields near Newton spilled over into the town. The Awbrey house, probably Buckingham Place in Glamorgan Street,[6] had suffered damage at the hands of the followers of Games, who were armed with a varied assortment of weapons such as javelins, forest bills and pikes. During the course of the court proceedings Games's retainers were asked whether 'on the said (5 December) (they had) assembled in Brecon and set upon (Sir William Awbrey and his servants) and pursued them into the house of William Awbrey, Doctor of Laws, Master of Requests, situated within the town of Brecknock . . . and threw stones over the wall or otherwise at the glass windows of the house, or assaulted the outer doors or walls of the gatehouse?' Naturally, the charges were denied, and John Games gave what was the standard answer to accusations of this kind, that the complaints were 'devised and imagined . . . to vex and molest (him) and put him to excessive costs and charges'.

Perhaps it would be as well to take our leave of Sir John and return to Brecon, for the afternoon shadows are getting longer. If time had permitted we could have continued along the A40 as far as Sennybridge before forking left to follow the A4067 to Dan-yr-ogof caves near Craig-y-nos. Here we could have visited the Welsh Jurassic Park with its giant reptiles and massive mammoths. Within the caves we would have seen depicted Stone Age man skinning his kill surrounded by members of his family. And the wild animals of that age are there; even the sabre-toothed tiger displaying his awesome strength. Outside, on the hillside, our imaginations would have been kindled by a representation of an Iron Age settlement, with domesticated animals, all built to half scale. But this has to be an ambition unfulfilled, for this is our last day. Tomorrow, we shall take our leave of the ancient borough, and though we shall shortly cease to feel the physical presence of the town, the memories and experiences will long remain with us, and contribute to making our lives richer and infinitely more satisfying. Who knows, some day we may well return, for there is so much still to see and so much still to learn. Our heritage, indeed, is one to be marvelled at, envied, and admired.

NOTES

[1] The others were: High Street Superior, High Street Inferior, Ship Street, St Mary's, Morgannwg, Cantref Selyf, Old Port Superior, Old Port Inferior, Watton, Heol Rydd and Trecastle.

[2] In a deposition about the state of Christ College **c.** 1582 it is stated that 'before the new B. [This is Bishop Middleton, bishop of St David's 1582-92] his coming to that Sea (sic) that Mr John Games had a window that was pulled down out of the college'.

[3] It read: John Games mab ag etifedd Hena Edward Games ap John ap Morgan ap Evan ap Dafydd Gam 1582 (John Games son and eldest heir of Edward Games son of John son of Morgan son of Evan son of Dafydd Gam 1582).

[4] Supra, p. 94-5.

[5] This step was reserved for serious contingencies such as murder or treason.

[6] Supra, p. 115-7.

Appendix
Genealogical Tree of the Watkinses of Penoyre

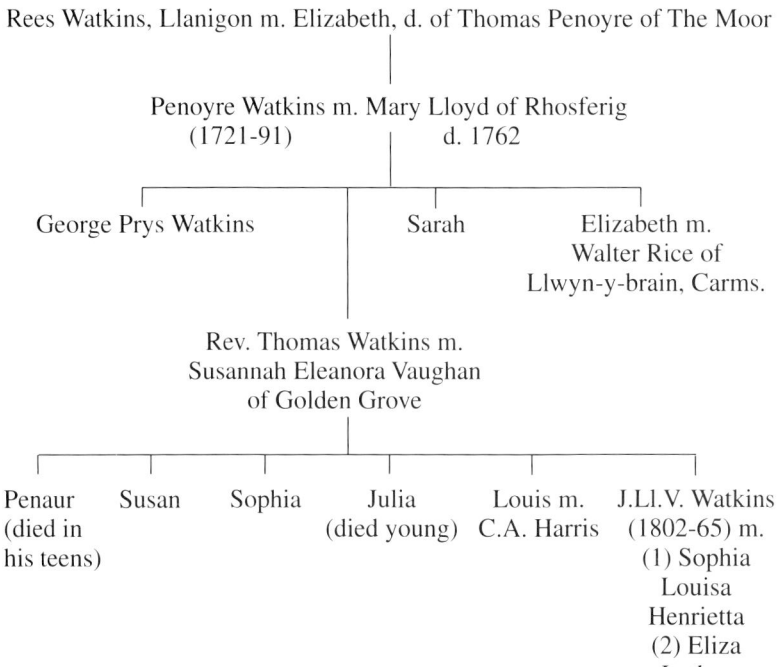

Rees Watkins, Llanigon m. Elizabeth, d. of Thomas Penoyre of The Moor

Penoyre Watkins m. Mary Lloyd of Rhosferig
(1721-91)   d. 1762

George Prys Watkins   Sarah   Elizabeth m.
Walter Rice of
Llwyn-y-brain, Carms.

Rev. Thomas Watkins m.
Susannah Eleanora Vaughan
of Golden Grove

Penaur   Susan   Sophia   Julia   Louis m.   J.Ll.V. Watkins
(died in   (died young) C.A. Harris   (1802-65) m.
his teens)   (1) Sophia
Louisa
Henrietta
(2) Eliza
Luther

Bibliography

A. *Background*

Atlas Brycheiniog, Llandysul, 1960.
Cambrensis, Giraldus, *The Itinerary Through Wales and the Description of Wales,* London, 1908.
Davies, John, *A History of Wales,* Penguin Books, 1994.
The Dictionary of Welsh Biography, Down to 1940, London, 1959.
Lloyd, John, *The Early History of the Old South Wales Iron Works,* London, 1906.
Peate, Iorwerth C., *The Welsh House,* Liverpool, 1946.
Roderick, A. J. (Ed.), *Wales Through the Ages,* Vol. 1, Llandybie, 1965.
Salter, Mike, *The Castles of Mid Wales,* Malvern, 1991.
Smith, L. T., (Ed.), *Leland's Itinerary in Wales,* London, 1906.
Smith, P., *Houses of the Welsh Countryside,* London, 1975.
Williams, Glanmor, *The Welsh Church from Conquest to Reformation,* Cardiff, 1976.

B. *Specific*

Books
Craster, O. E., *Brecon Gaer, Aberyscir, Breconshire,* West Bromwich, 1954.
Hutchinson, F. E., *Henry Vaughan: A Life and Interpretation,* Oxford, 1947.
Jones, Theophilus, *History of the County of Brecknock,* Ed. J. R. Bailey, Brecknock, 1909.
Parry, E. G., *Christ College Brecon: An Illustrated History,* Pontypool, 1991.
Poole, Edwin, *The Illustrated History and Biography of Brecknockshire from the Earliest Times to the Present Day,* Brecon, 1886.
Pritchard, Elsie, *Penoyre,* Brecon, 1969.
Id., *Brecon From the Struet,* Brecon, 1977.
Radford, C. A. Ralegh, (Revised and Edited by Robinson, D. M.), *Tretower Court and Castle,* London, 1990.
Thomas, W. S. K., *Brecon, 1093-1660,* Llandysul, 1991.
Id., *Georgian and Victorian Brecon,* Llandysul, 1993.
Id., *Footprints in the Sand: Brecknock Notabilities,* Llandysul, 1994.
The Cathedral Church of St John the Evangelist, Brecon, Royal Commission on the Ancient and Historical Monuments of Wales, Brecon, 1994.
Wheeler, R. E. Mortimer, *The Roman Fort Near Brecon,* London, 1926.
Williamson, E. W., *Henry Vaughan,* Cardiff, 1953.

Articles

Bacon O. L., 'Mason's Marks in Brecon Cathedral', *Brycheiniog*, 25 (1992-3).

Cathcart, King, D. J., 'The Castles of Breconshire', *Brycheiniog*, 7 (1961).

Clark, G. T., 'Bronllys Castle', *Arch. Camb.*, VIII (1862).

Id., 'Some Remarks upon Bronllys Tower', *Arch. Camb.*, XII (1866).

Davies, Dewi, 'The County Gaol in Brecon', *Brycheiniog*, XXV (1992-3).

Dumbleton, E. N., 'On a Crannoge, or stockaded island, in Llangorse Lake, near Brecon', *Arch. Camb.*, 1 (1870).

Fox, Cyril, 'Canoe Discovered in Llangorse Lake', *Arch. Camb.*, V (1925).

Jones, E. P., 'Cartrefi Enwogion Sir Frycheiniog', *Brycheiniog*, 13 (1968-9).

Jones, S. R. and Smith, J. T., 'The Houses of Breconshire', Part III, *Brycheiniog*, II (1965).

Minchinton, W. E., 'The Place of Brecknock in the Industrialisation of South Wales', *Brycheiniog*, 7 (1961).

Parry, E. G., 'Newton and its Owners, 1582-1725', *Arch. Camb.*, 133 (1984).

Id., 'Llyn Llan-gors: The Historical Background', *Brycheiniog*, 22 (1986-7).

Id., 'The Castle of Brecon Hotel', *Brycheiniog*, XXV (1992-3).

Pritchard, Elsie, 'Gwenllian Morgan (1852-1939)', *Brycheiniog*, 12 (1966-7).

Radford, C. A. Ralegh, 'Tretower: The Castle and the Court', *Brycheiniog*, 6 (1960).

Redwood, Pamela, 'The Games Family versus the Borough of Brecon, 1589-1606', *Brycheiniog*, XXV (1992-3).

Savory, H. N., 'Prehistoric Brecknock', *Brycheiniog*, 1 (1955).

Sayce, R. W., 'Hill Top Camps', *Cymmrodorion Soc. Trans.*, 1920-21.

Smith, J. Beverley, 'Llywelyn ap Gruffudd and the March of Wales', *Brycheiniog*, 20 (1982-3).

Smith, Llinos Beverley, 'The Death of Llywelyn ap Gruffydd: The Narratives Reconsidered', *Welsh Hist. Rev.*, II (1982-3).

Thomas, J. D. H., 'Llywelyn y Llyw Olaf', *Brycheiniog*, 2 (1956).

Index

Caratacus (Caradog), 5
Carmarthen, xvii, 7, 63, 102, 140
Caröe, W. D., 92
castles: Brecon, xiv, 17, 44, 87, 88, 91, 98, 99-111, 116, 146; Bronllys,
    xiv, 57-60, 104; Tretower, xiv, 23, 38-41, 42, 45, 47
cavalry (Vettonian), 7, 9, 11
caves (Dan-yr-ogof), xiii, 159
Celts, xiii, 1, 5, 30; Celtic Church (*clas*), xiii, 13-15, 34
Charles I (1625-49), xv, 46, 71, 96, 97, 108, 113
Charles II (1660-85), 17; prince, 96
Chartists, 25
Cherry, Andrew (Actor), 23-4
Chester, xiv, 5, 7, 46, 63, 64
Christ College. *See under* schools.
Churchyard, Thomas (Poet), 116, 133
Cilmery, xv, 41, 49, 60, 66, 104
Cleasby, Sir Anthony, 79-80
Cleasby, Richard Digby, 80
Coke, Dr Thomas, 85, 125, 143
Council in Wales and the Marches, 71, 95, 108, 158
courts: Assize, xvii, 80, 127, 129, 130, 131, 149, 150; Baron, 17, 109;
    Great Sessions, 46, 109, 127, 151; Leet, 17, 109-110, 136; Petty Sessions,
    129; Quarter Sessions, 72, 80, 127, 128, 130, 134, 135, 156; Star
    Chamber, 156
County House, 130
Cradoc, xvi, 5, 75, 82, 83, 86
Craig-y-nos, xiii, 81, 128
crannog, xiii, 30-3, 34
Cromwell, Oliver, xv, 96
Cromwell, Thomas, 139

David, Bishop of St David's, 18, 58
David, Richard (Prior), 139, 140
Davies, Edward (Rev.), 143
Derby, Abraham, 56
drovers (porthmyn), xvi, 49, 68-73

Edward I (1272-1307), 41, 64-5, 66, 104, 138; prince, 63, 103
Edward II (1307-27), 104
Edward III (1327-77), 106
Edward IV (1461-83), 106
Edward VI (1547-53), 16
Edwards, Thomas, 134-5

166

walls: Brecon town, 98, 105, 112-5, 120, 135; Antonine, 9; Hadrian, 9
Ward, John (Actor), xvi
Watkins, George Pryce, 75
Watkins, Col. J. Lloyd Vaughan (M.P.), xv, 76-9, 150
Watkins, Penoyre, 75
Watkins, Thomas (Rev.), 75-6, 79
Watson, John Boles, 23
Watton, xvi, 23, 25, 80, 110, 112, 117, 135, 147
Wellington, Richard, 55
William de Barri, 18
Williams, Sir David (of Gwernyfed), 156-7
Williams, Deiniol, 86
Williams, John (Archbishop), 71
Winton, John Parry de, 79, 130
Winton, William Seymour, 98
Wise, Catherine, 46, 48n
Worcester, Treaty of (1218), 102
Wolsey, Thomas (Cardinal), 111
Wood, Thomas (M.P.), 77, 96-7, 144
Wyatt, T. H., 92, 128
Wynne, Ellis, 72

Yny Lhyvyr Hwnn (1546), xv, 95